## Second Edition
# Cambridge Little Steps 2

**Activity Book**
Gabriela Zapiain

# Contents

1. What do you like to do at school?   3
2. How can we take care of ourselves?   17
3. What do we do at home?   31
4. What can we see on a farm?   45
5. What meals do we eat?   59
6. What clothes do we wear?   73
7. What can we do with our senses?   87
8. How do we travel?   101
9. What do plants need to grow?   115

Picture Dictionary   129

Stickers

# 1. What do you like to do at school?

👆 Point.  ⬤ Stick.  ✏️ Color.  👄 Say.

cut

paint

glue

color

draw

**Vocabulary:** *paint, draw, color, cut, glue.* Say each new word, and children point to each action as you say it. Say: *(Paint / Draw).* Stick *(paint / draw).* Children stick each sticker as you say it. Then name the other actions. Children color each action as you say it. Finally, children point to and name each action. Optional: Children trace the initial letter of each word, while repeating the word.

 Say. Color.

Story

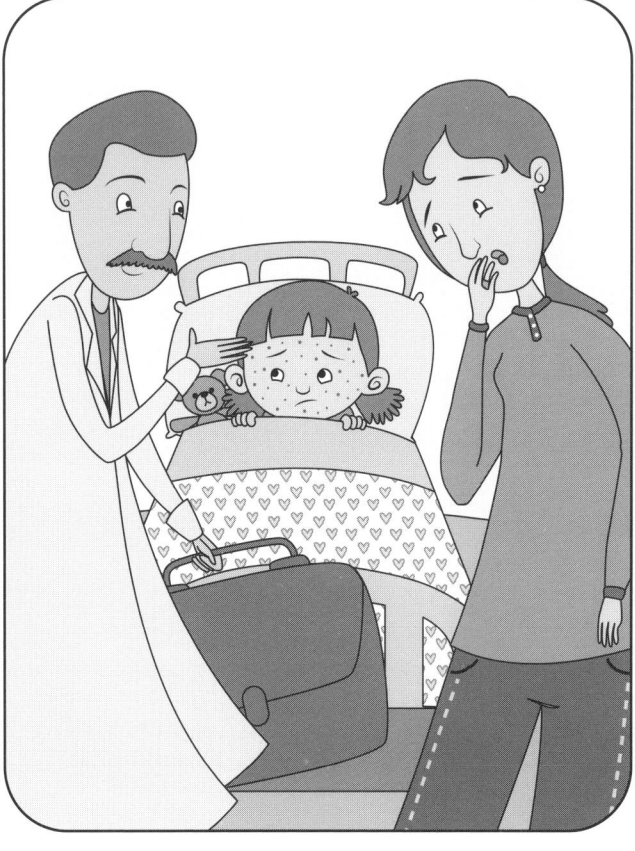

**Language: Betty is (sad). sad, happy.** Ask children to remember the story. Point to each scene from the story and have children say: *Betty is sad. / Betty is happy.* They color the sad or happy faces, depending on how Betty is feeling in each scene.

 Phonics

Bb

Hh

Mm

Ss

Tt

**Phonics:** *b*ook /b/, *h*ouse /h/, *m*ouse /m/, *s*ad /s/, *t*eacher /t/. Point to each letter and say the sounds /b/, /h/, /m/, /s/, /t/. Children repeat. Then point to each picture and say the word. Children repeat. Point to the first letter, and say the sound. Then, using your finger, trace the line from the letter to the picture and say the sound and the word together for children to repeat. Children trace the lines to match each letter to its picture, then point and say the sounds and words. They follow the letters with their fingers. Optional: Children trace the letters with a pencil.

 Literacy

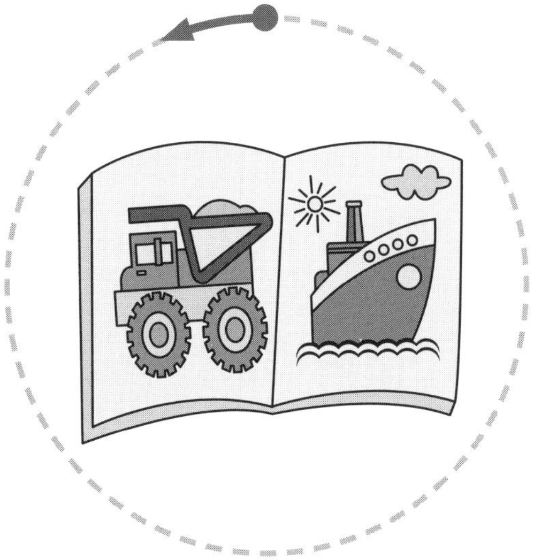

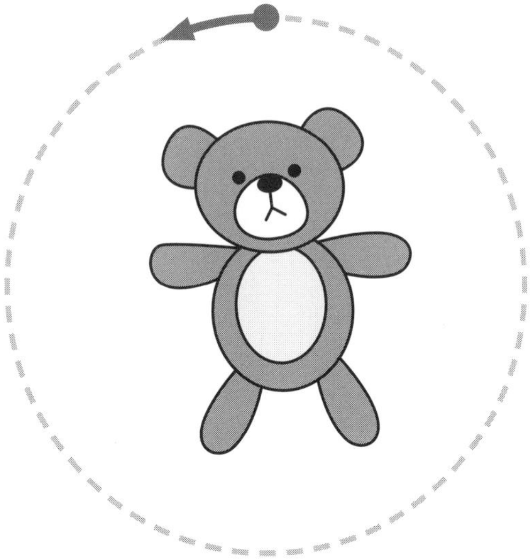

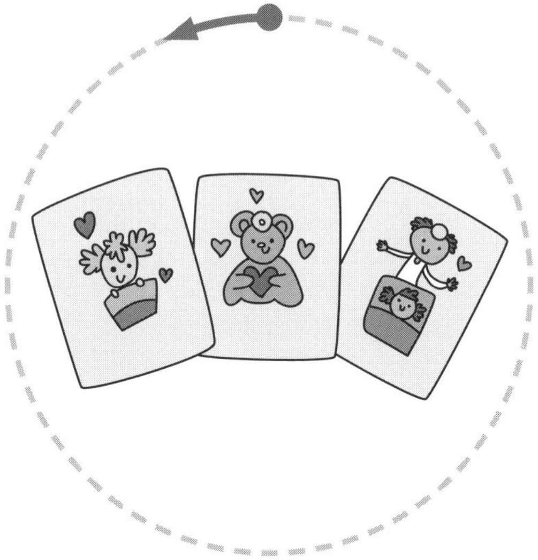

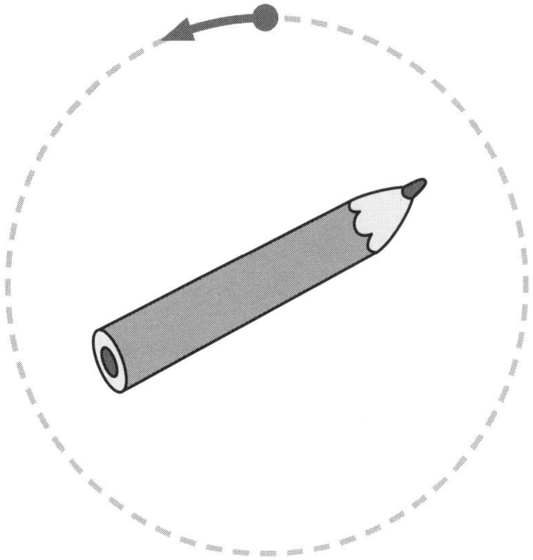

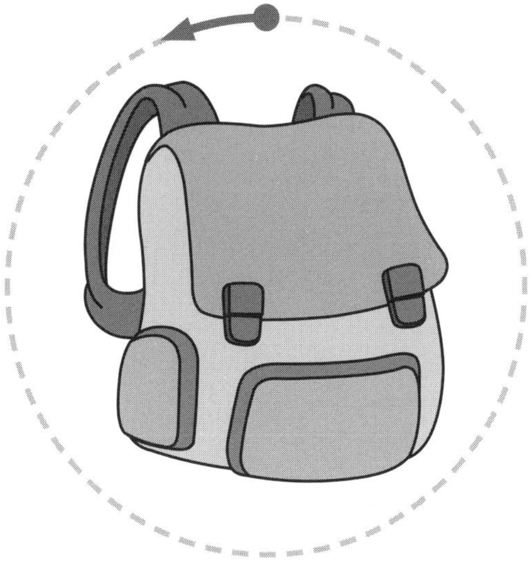

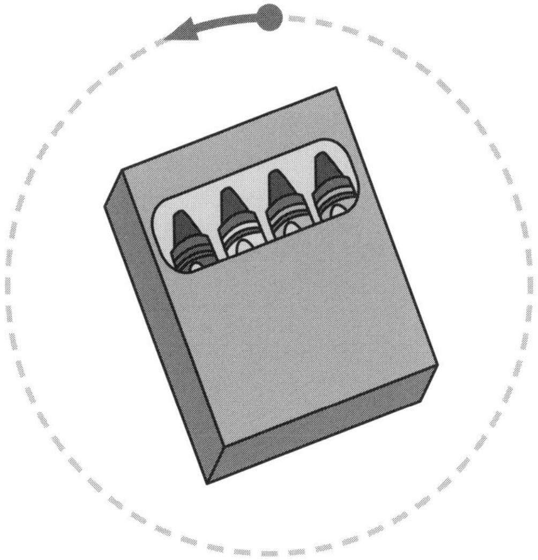

Do you like the story?

**Literacy: Identifying details about a character.** Ask: *Can you remember the presents Betty received in the story? Which are Betty's presents?* Children point to, name, and circle Betty's presents (*coloring book, cards, and crayons*). Finally, ask: *Do you like the story? (Yes. / No.)* Children color the happy face or the sad face.

# Look. Color. Say.

Values

**Values: Cleaning up the classroom.** Children look at the scene. Point to one of the children cleaning up and ask: *What's he / she doing? (Cleaning up the classroom.)* Then point to a child who isn't cleaning up and ask: *Is he / she cleaning up the classroom?* Discuss why not and what the child could do better. Finally, children identify and color the children who are cleaning up the classroom. Encourage them to say: *(He's) cleaning up.*

Unit 1  7

 Look.  Match. Say.

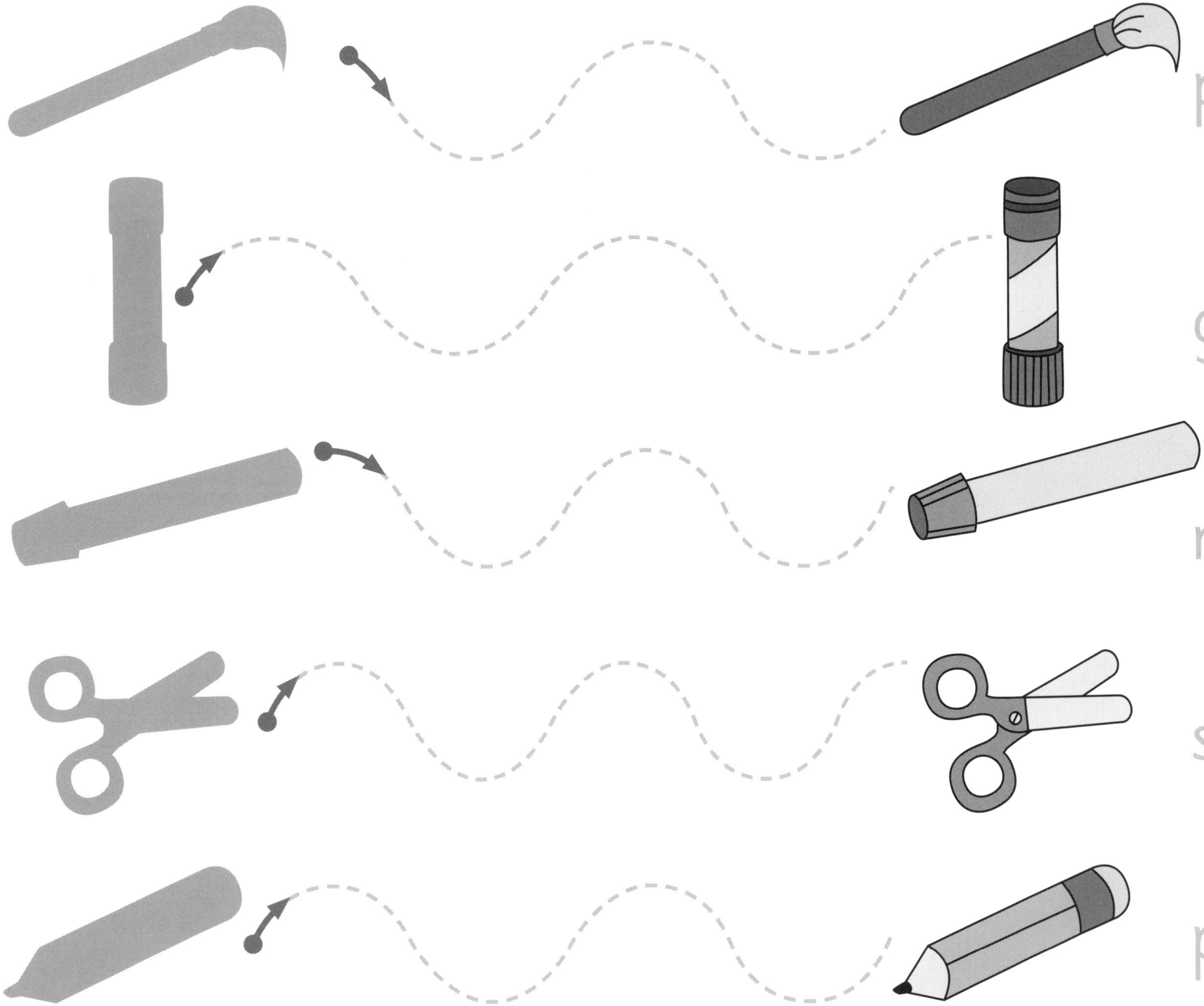

Vocabulary

paintbrush

glue stick

marker

scissors

pencil

**Vocabulary:** *pencil, marker, paintbrush, glue stick, scissors.* Children point to the items in the second column and name each one. Then, they trace the lines to match the silhouettes on the left to the items on the right. Finally, they finger trace the lines and name the items as they link the pictures. Optional: Children trace the initial letters of each word.

 Count. Say. Color.

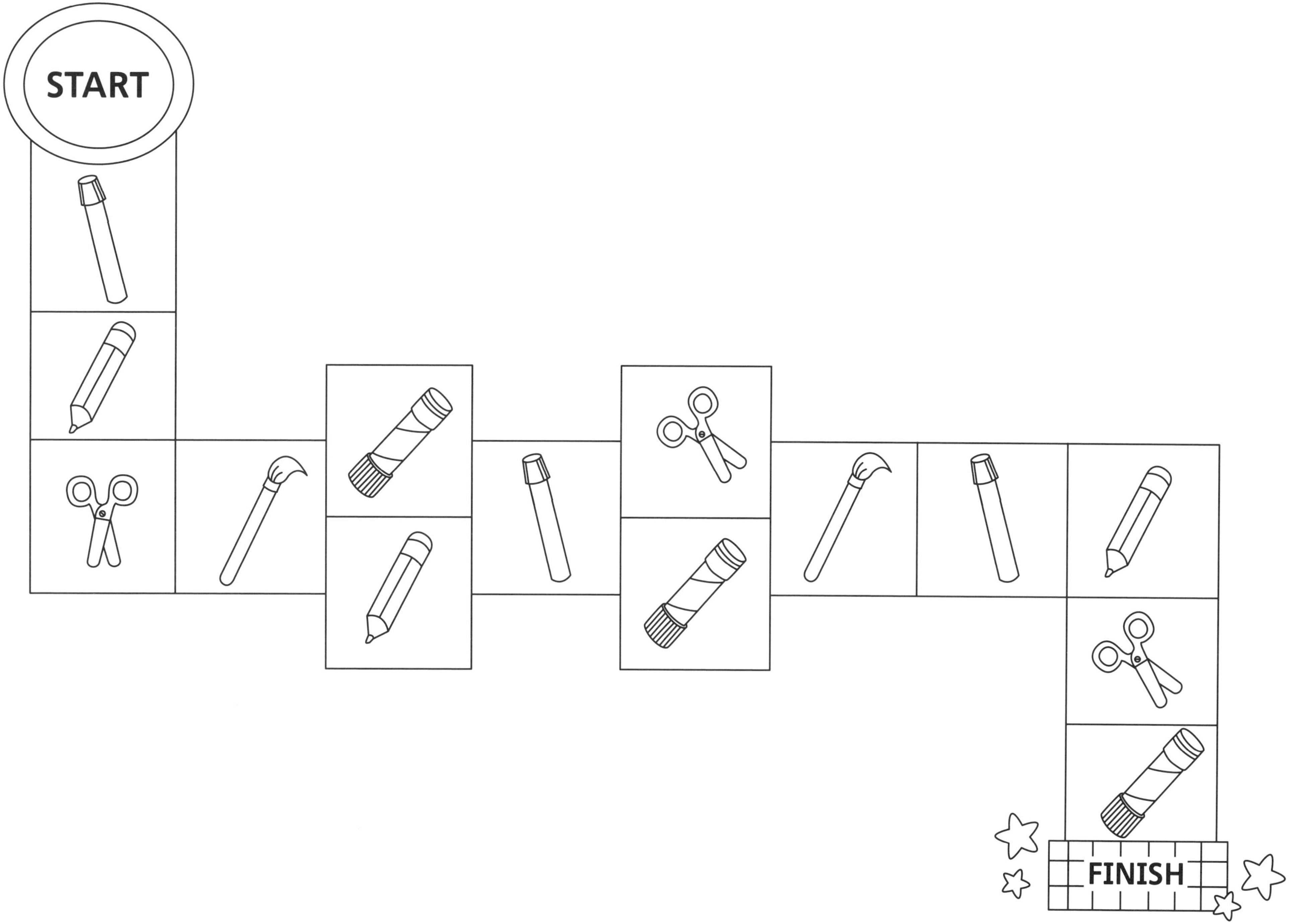

Language

**Language:** *I (draw) with (a pencil).* Look at the game together. Identify the start and finish places and then demonstrate how to roll a dice, count, and move the corresponding number of squares. Explain that, when children land on a square, they must name the object, say what they do with the object, and then color it. Model a few times, saying: *I (draw) with (a pencil). I cut with (scissors).* Distribute crayons and dice, then guide and support children as they play in groups.

Unit 1  9

# ✏️ Color. 👄 Say.

Concept

**Concept: Expressing color preferences.** Distribute crayons in the six colors from the Student's Book page (red, blue, yellow, green, orange, purple). Say a color, and children hold up the correct crayon. They then use it to color one of the paint blobs at the top of the page. Repeat with all the colors. Point to the (pencil). Ask: *What's this? What color is the (pencil)?* Explain that children can color it any color from the six at the top of the page. Repeat with the other objects, explaining that children should choose a different color for each object. When they finish coloring, children point to the objects on the page and say: *My (pencil) is (blue)*.

 Say. ✓ Check.

Vocabulary

listen to stories

play with friends

clean up

eat lunch

sing songs

**Vocabulary:** *listen to stories, play with friends, clean up, eat lunch, sing songs.* Point to each activity and encourage children to repeat as you name each of them. Ask: *What do you do at school?* Children respond by pointing or saying: *I (sing songs at school).* Children check the activities they do at school. Optional: Children trace the initial letters of each phrase.

Unit 1 · 11

 Say.  Draw.  Match.

Language

**Language:** *What do you like to do? I like to (clean up).* Ask: *What do you like to do at school?* Allow several children to answer by pointing to the pictures or by saying, e.g., *I like to sing songs. I like to color with markers. I like to play with friends.* Children draw and color the child in the center of the page to look like themselves looking happy. Then, they draw lines from this to the activities they like to do. Finally, they present their work and say: *I like to (sing).*

# Say. Match. Draw.

 Speaking

May I get some paper, please?

May I go to the bathroom, please?

May I have some water, please?

**Language:** *May I (get some paper), please? Yes, you may.* Point to the first two pictures on the left, read the questions, and have children repeat after you. Allow several children to ask the questions, and respond each time with: *Yes, you may.* Then, they look at the first two pictures and draw lines to match each character to what he or she needs. Repeat with the third picture. Children draw a line to match the character to the box on the right, then draw a picture of what she needs (*water*). Then, children work in pairs and take turns asking and aswering the questions.

Unit 1    13

 Look.  Color.  Stick. Say.

Cross-curricular: Art

yellow

red

blue

**Art: Identifying primary colors.** Ask: *What are the primary colors? (Red, blue, yellow.)* Children look at the pictures. Ask: *What color is the sun? (Yellow.)* Repeat with the other pictures. Children color each picture the correct color. Distribute magazines, scissors, and glue. Children find and cut out pictures of yellow, red, and blue things, and stick them in the correct column. Alternatively, children could draw and color things of theirs that are these colors. When they're finished, children can present their pages, pointing and saying: *It's red. It's blue. It's yellow.*

**Trace.**  **Count.** **Color.**

**Numeracy**

1 2 3 4 5 6 7 8 9 10

⑦  ⑨    ⑧  ⑩

**Numeracy:** *one, two, three, four, five, six, seven, eight, nine, ten.* Lead children in counting to 10. Children trace the numbers. Ask: *How many crayons? Let's count!* Children count the crayons in each box, and color the correct number for each box. Help children count and choose ten crayons and use them to color the crayons.

 Say. Circle. Draw. Color.   Review

## What do you like to do at school?

**My favorite thing in Unit 1:**

Unit 1

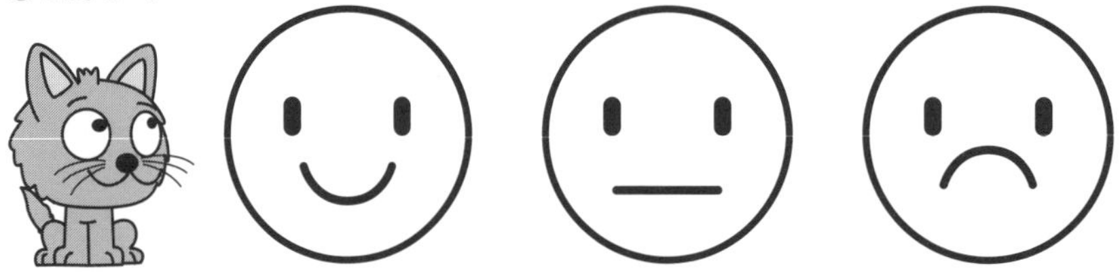

**Vocabulary and Language Review:** Ask the Big Question: *What do you like to do at school?* Children look back through Unit 1 to recall what they have learned. Ask them to look at the eight pictures from Unit 1. They say the words and circle the pictures they are able to name. Then ask: *What was your favorite thing in this unit?* Remind children of the song, story, cross-curricular lesson, etc. They draw a picture of their favorite thing. Children point to and talk about their pictures. Answer the Big Question together, using their pictures as a prompt. Finally, focus on the self-assessment activity. Ask: *How did you do in this unit?* Children color the face that shows how they feel they did.

# 2 How can we take care of ourselves?

 Point.  Stick.  Color. Say.

wash my face

drink water

eat healthy food

put on a jacket

brush my hair

**Vocabulary:** *wash my face, brush my hair, eat healthy food, put on a jacket, drink water.* Say each new phrase, and children point to each action as you say it. Say: *(Eat Healthy food / Put on a jacket). Stick (eat healthy food / put on a jacket).* Children stick each sticker as you say it. Then name the other actions. Children color each action as you say it. Finally, children point to and name each action. Optional: Children trace the initial letter of each phrase, while repeating the phrase.

# 👁 Look. ⭕ Circle. ✏ Color.  Story

**Language:** *What can you see? jacket.* Ask children to remember the story. Then ask them to circle four differences between the pictures (in the second he has messy hair, a dirty face, slippers, and no jacket). Finally, children color the circle of the picture that is from the story.

 **Look.**  **Say.**  **Circle.**  **Follow.**

**Phonics**

# Ff  Gg  Jj  Kk  Ll

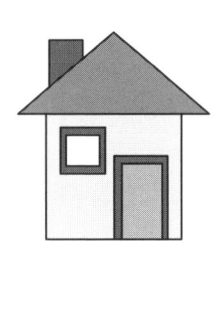

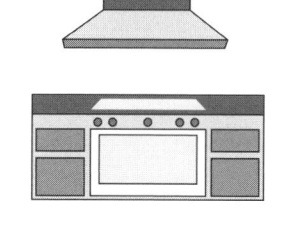

**Phonics:** *f*ace /f/, *g*oodbye /g/, *j*acket /ʤ/, *k*itchen /k/, *l*unchbox /l/. Point to the first letter and say the sound /f/. Children repeat. Then point to each picture under it and say the word. Say: *F- f- Which word? (Face.)* Show children how to circle the face. Repeat with the other letters, sounds, and words. Children circle the correct picture for each letter, then point and say the sounds and words. They follow the letters with their fingers. Optional: Children trace the letters with a pencil.

Unit 2

✓ Check.  Say. ✏ Color.

Literacy

Do you like the story?

 Unit 2

**Literacy: Identifying a character's actions in a story.** Ask: *Can you remember what Oliver does in the story?* Point to the first picture and ask: *What's this? Does he do this in the story?* Children answer *yes* or *no*. Repeat with the other pictures. Children check the box next to each action that Oliver does in the story. Finally, ask: *Do you like the story? (Yes. / No.)* Children color the happy face or the sad face.

 **Look.**  **Say.**   **Point.**   **Match.**

Values

**Values: Taking care of ourselves.** Point to the first child on the left. Ask: *What can she do to take care of herself? (Drink water.)* Children find and point to the girl drinking water on the right. They draw a line to match the pictures. Repeat with the other pictures.

Unit 2 | 21

 Look. Match. Say.

Vocabulary

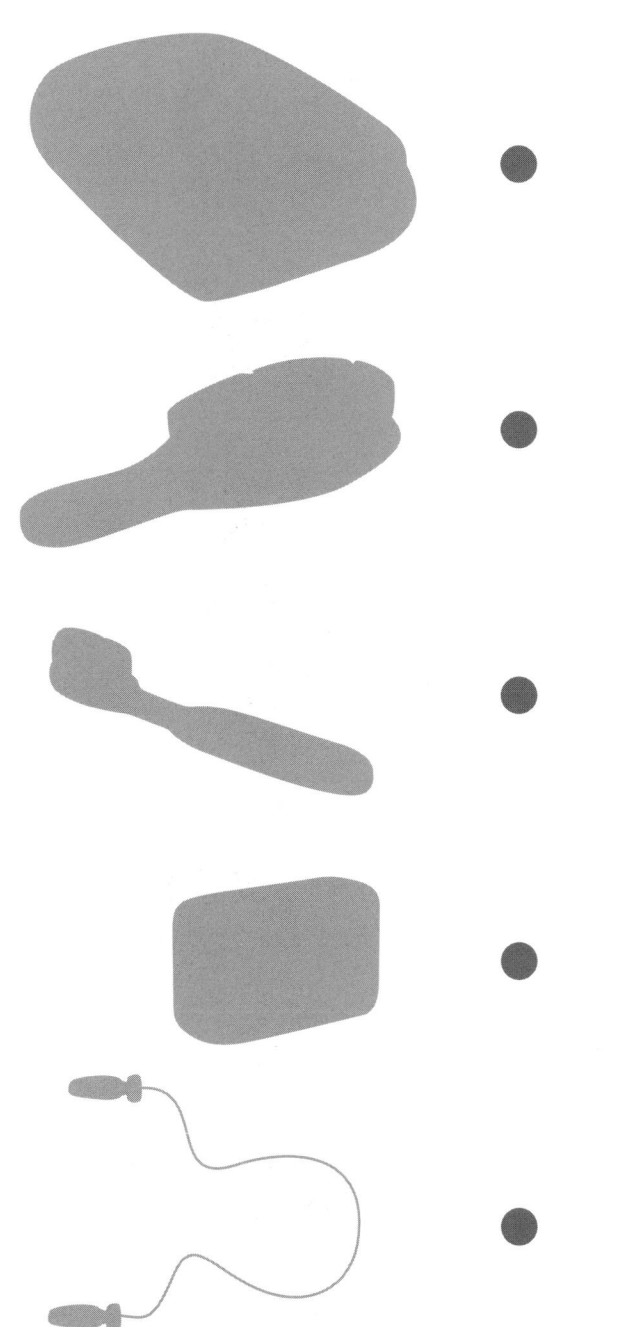

 brush

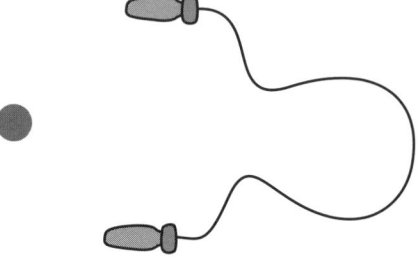 jump rope

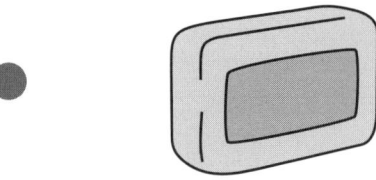 soap

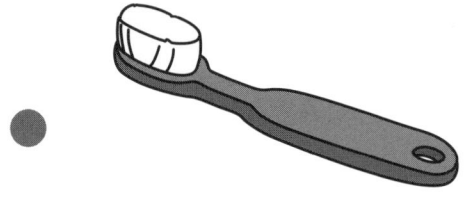 toothbrush

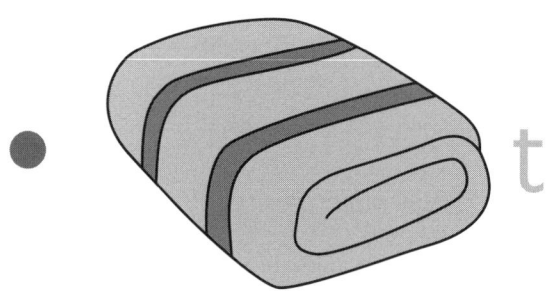 towel

**Vocabulary:** *soap, brush, toothbrush, towel, jump rope.* Children point to the items in the second column and name each one. Then, they draw lines to match the silhouettes on the left to the items on the right. Finally, they finger trace the lines and name the items as they match the pictures. Optional: Children trace the initial letters of each word.

 Look. Point. Circle. Say.　　　　Language

 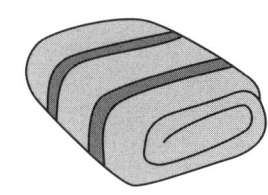 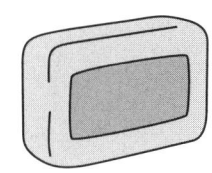 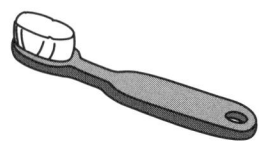 

  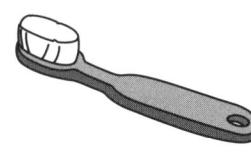 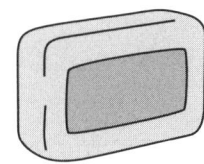 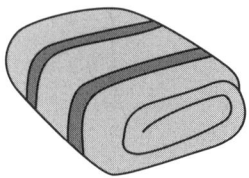

 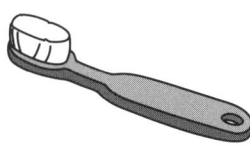 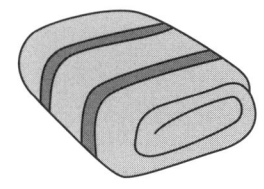  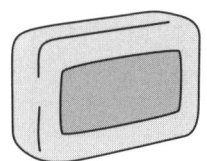

 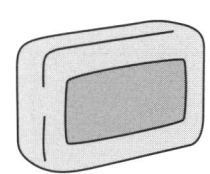  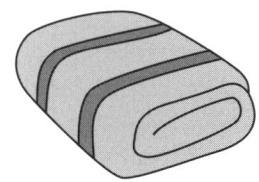 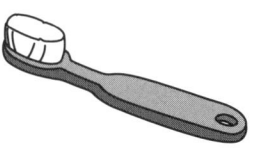

**Language:** *She washes her hands with soap. He dries his hair with a towel. He / She brushes his / her (teeth) with a (toothbrush).* Children point to and name each action and each object. Point to the first child, and say: *She washes her hands with …?* Children point to the soap, circle it, and complete the sentence. They find and circle the object that the child is using in each row, then talk about each child.

Unit 2　23

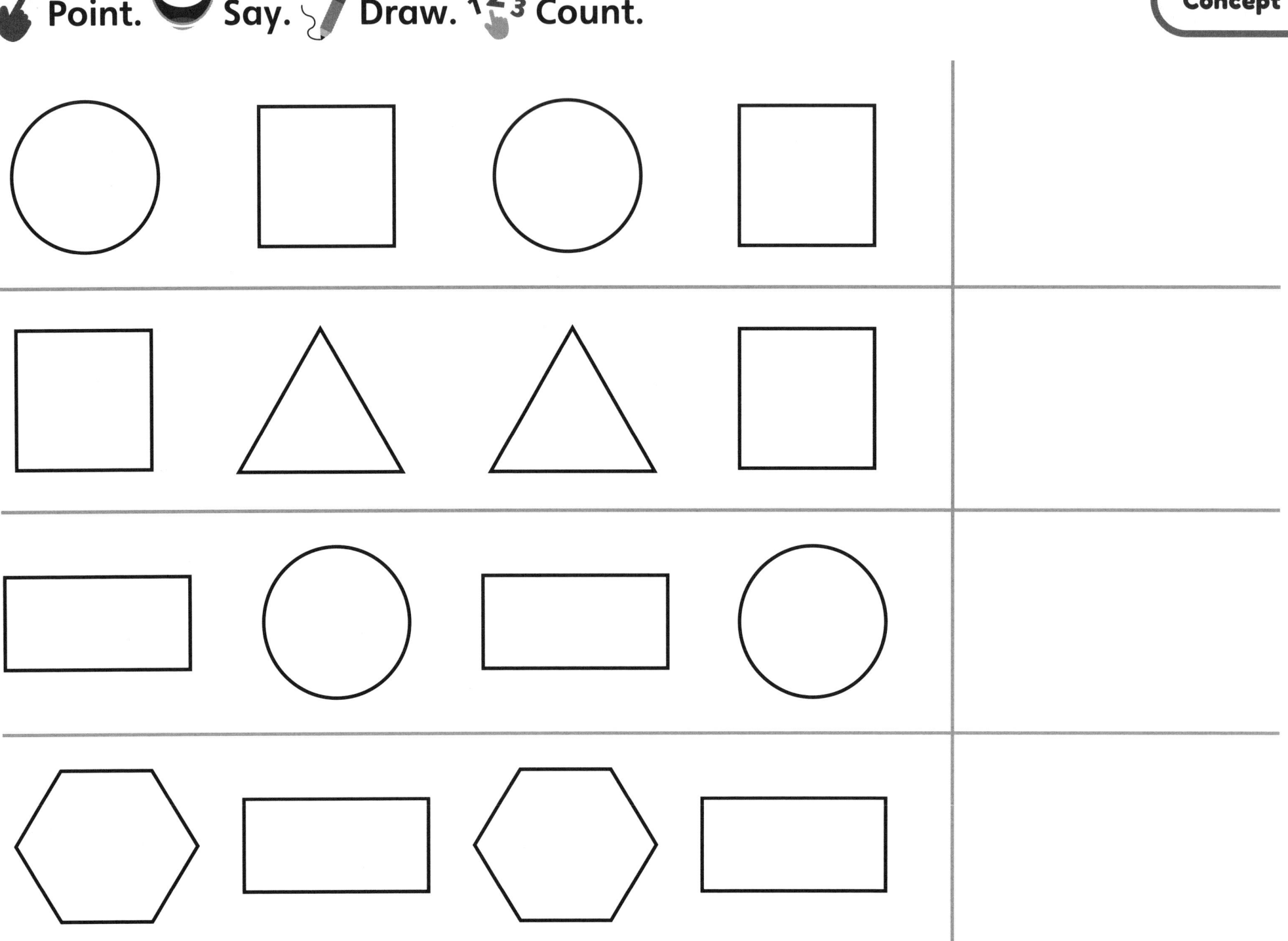

**Concept: Identifying the properties of shapes.** Children point to and name each shape. Then, they look at the pattern in each row and say what shape should come next. Guide them through the first row. Say: *Circle, square, circle, square ... What comes next? (Circle.)* Children draw a circle in the empty space. Continue with the other rows. Once children have finished drawing, ask them to repeat the completed patterns. Then ask them to count the corners of the shapes they have drawn.

 **Look.**  **Match.**  **Say.**

**Vocabulary**

thirsty

tired

dirty

hungry

sick

**Vocabulary:** *tired, thirsty, dirty, hungry, sick.* Point to the first emoji and say: *I'm …? (Thirsty.)* Point to the children and cat at the bottom of the page and ask: *Who's thirsty?* Children say *thirsty* and draw a line to match the emoji to the thirsty child. Repeat with the other emojis and children / cat. Finally, children point and say each word. Optional: Children trace the initial letters of each word.

 Look.  Say.  Circle.

Language

**Language:** *What's the matter? She's / He's (tired). What can he / she do? He / She can (sleep).* Point to the first picture and say: *What's the matter? (She's tired.)* Direct children's attention to the two choices and ask: *What can she do? She can …?* Children say the correct answer *(sleep)* and then circle it. Repeat with the other pictures, asking the question, eliciting and repeating the answer, and then allowing children time to circle.

## 👁 Look. ✨ Match. 👄 Say.

**Speaking**

"I'm hungry."

"I'm thirsty."

**Language:** *I'm (hungry). You need to (eat)!* Point to Leo on the left and say: *I'm hungry!* Children repeat, and mime being hungry. Point to the two children on the right, and ask: *Who can help Leo? (Mia.) What does Mia say? You need to eat!* Children repeat and mime handing over an apple. Children draw a line between hungry Leo and Mia. Repeat with thirsty Mia. Divide the class into two groups, and tell one group they are Mia and the other group they are Leo. Explain that children will act out the dialogues. Point to hungry Leo, then Mia with the apple, and children say the lines. Repeat with the other pictures. Repeat several times with large and small groups of children. You could invite confident children to come to the front and act Leo or Mia with you as the other character.

## Think. Circle. Color. Draw.

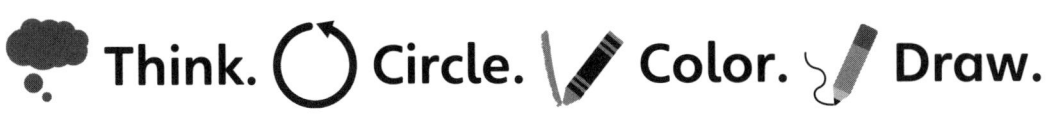

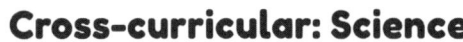

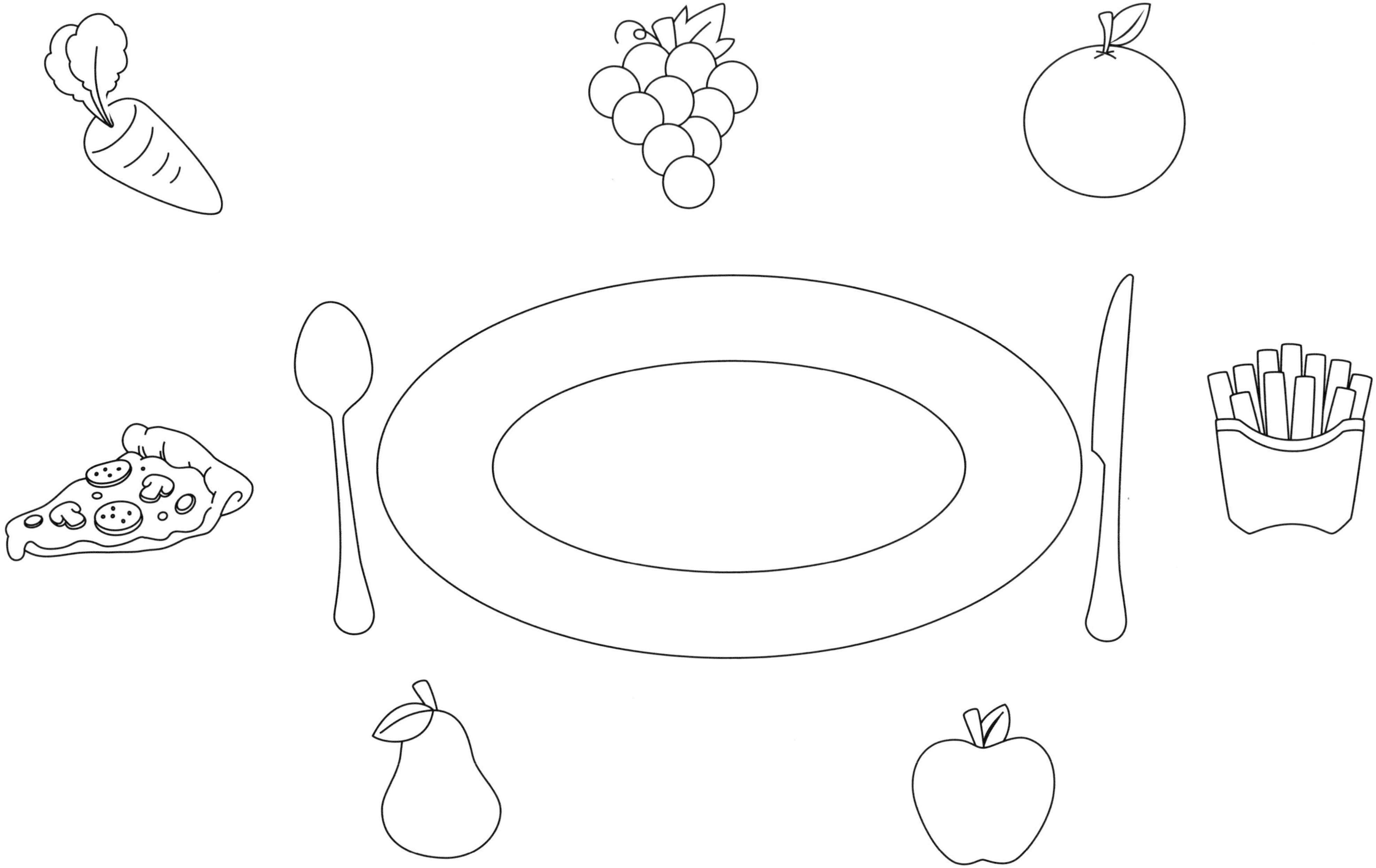

**Science: Learning to recognize healthy food.** Ask children to look at all the food and say: *Can you see any food that we can eat every day?* Children circle the food that we can eat every day (carrot, grapes, orange, pear, and apple). Then point to the slice of pizza and the French fries and ask: *Can we eat this food every day?* Accept all children's opinions and ideas. Children can also color the food they like. Then say: *Let's eat some food!* Children plan and draw a meal, including food they can eat every day as well as food they can eat sometimes.

 Trace.  Count. Match. Color.

**Numeracy**

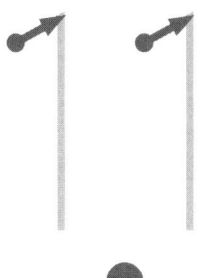 

Numeracy: *eleven*, *twelve*. Lead children in counting to 12. They trace the numbers 11 and 12. Point to the first jacket and say: *How many stars? Let's count!* Repeat with the second jacket. Children match the numbers to the jackets. They can then color the stars.

Unit 2 — 29

 Say. Circle. Draw. Color.

Review

## How can we take care of ourselves?

**My favorite thing in Unit 2:**

**Unit 2**

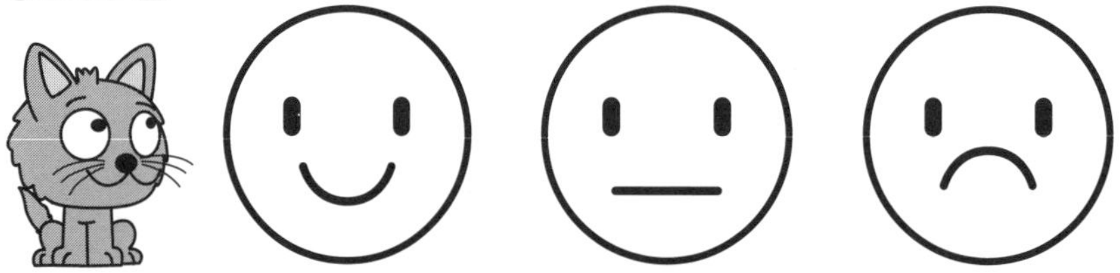

# 3 What do we do at home?

 Point.  Stick.  Color.  Say.

kitchen

dining room

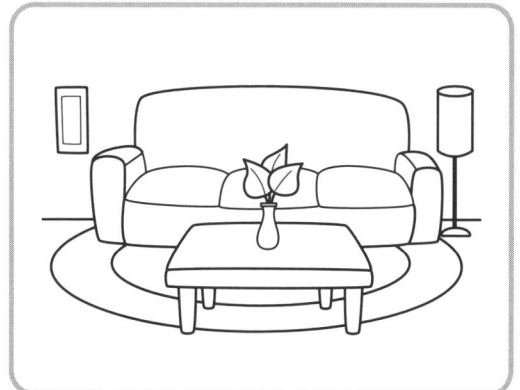
living room

bedroom

bathroom

**Vocabulary:** *living room, dining room, kitchen, bedroom, bathroom.* Say each new word, and children point to each room as you say it. *Say: (Dining room / Bathroom). Stick the (dining room / bathroom).* Children stick each sticker as you say it. Then name the other rooms. Children color each room as you say it. Finally, children point to and name each room. Optional: Children trace the initial letter of each word, while repeating the word.

 **Match. Say.**

Story

**Language:** *Where is (the cat)? (The cat) is in the (bedroom).* Ask children to remember the story. Point to each room and have children say the name of the room. Then point to the cat. Ask: *Where is the cat in the story?* Children answer: *The cat is in the bedroom.* They draw a line to match the cat to the correct room. Repeat for the father and mother.

 **Look.**  **Say.**  **Match.**  **Follow.**

**Phonics**

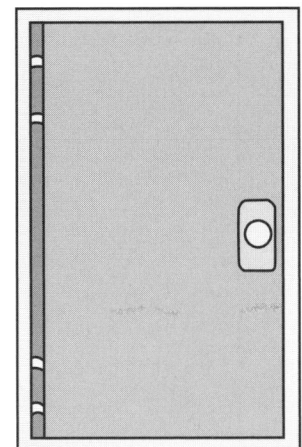

Cc
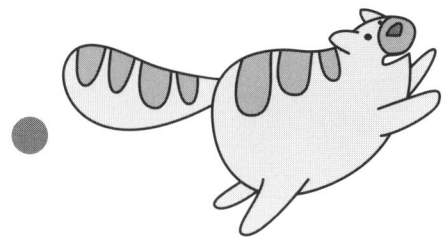

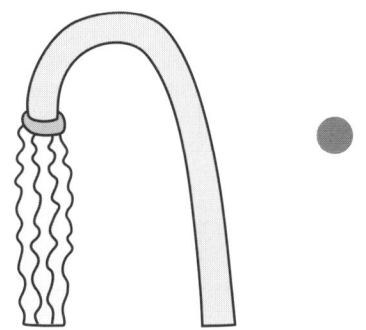

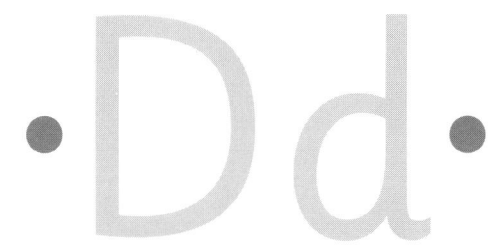
Dd
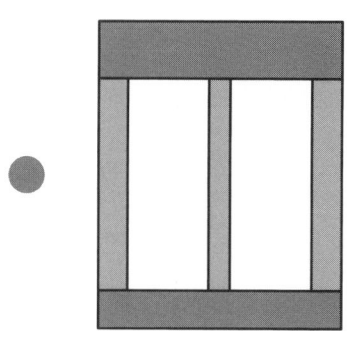

Ww

**Phonics:** *c*andy /k/, *d*oor /d/, *w*ater /w/. Point to each letter and say the sounds /k/, /d/, /w/. Children repeat. Then point to each picture and say the word. Children repeat. Point to the first letters and say: *K- k- Which words? (Candy. / Cat.)* Children draw lines to match the letters to the correct pictures, then point to and say the sounds and words. Repeat with the other letters, sounds, and words. Children draw lines to match the pictures and letters, then point and say the sounds and words. Finally, children follow the letters with their finger. Optional: Children trace the letters with a pencil.

Unit 3 33

 Say. Draw. Color.

Literacy

Do you like the story?

**Literacy: Identifying scenes from a story.** Children look at the scene. Ask: *Can you remember? Is this a scene from the story?* Allow children to notice that the cat (Tabby) is missing. Ask: *What's missing?* Children describe the cat, where it is, and what it is doing in the story (sleeping in its cat bed). Children draw the cat in the right place. They can then color the scene to match the story, using the same colors. Finally, ask: *Do you like the story? (Yes. / No.)* Children color the happy face or the sad face.

Unit 3

 Draw. Say.

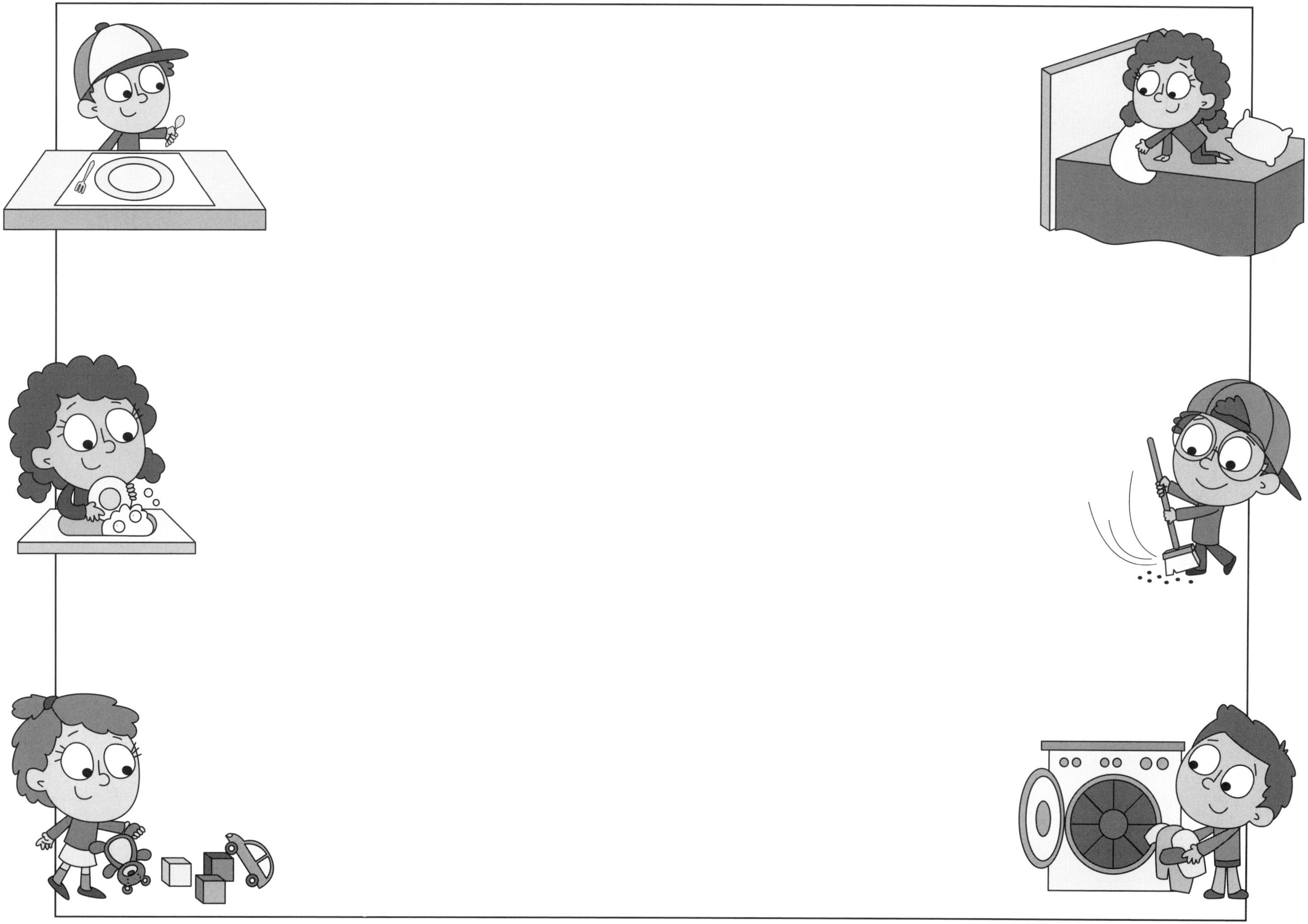

Values

**Values: Helping at home.** Point to the pictures and ask children what they do in each room to help at home. Have a discussion about what things children do to help at home. Children draw themselves helping. They point and say: *I help at home.*

Unit 3 35

 Say. Count. Write.

Vocabulary

bed

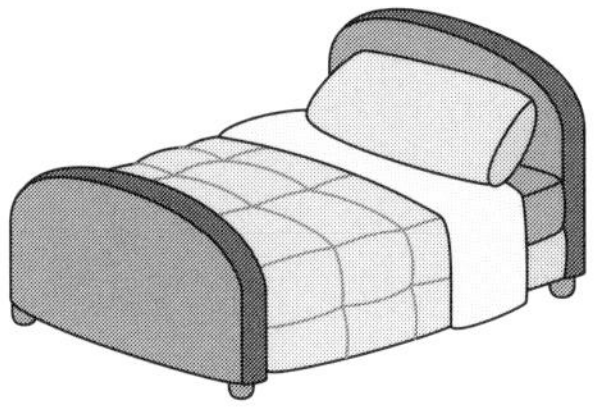

shower

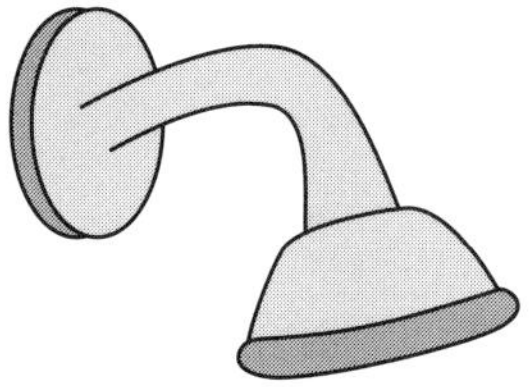

couch

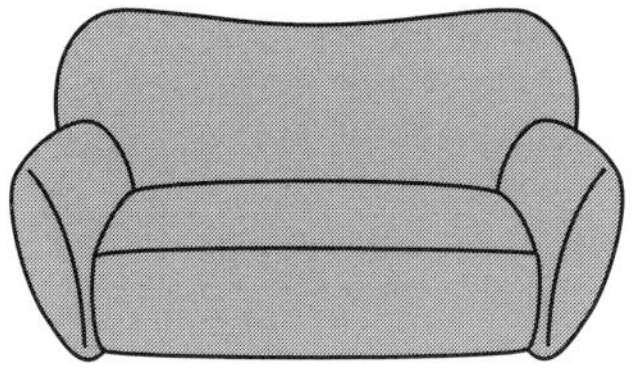

lamp

fridge

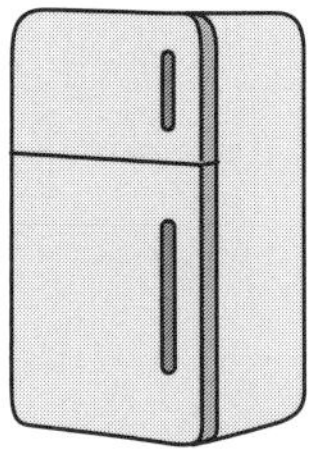

**Vocabulary:** *shower, bed, couch, lamp, fridge.* Children look at the pictures in the left column and name each item. Then, they search for each item inside the house and count them. Finally, say together: *How many beds? Three! Three beds.* Children write the number next to each item. Optional: They trace the initial letter of each word.

Unit 3

 **Look. Check. Say.**

**Language**

**Language:** *Where does the (shower) go? The (shower) goes in the (bathroom).* Point to each object in the first column and children name them. Then look at the rooms in the top row. Point to the couch. Ask: *Where does it go? In the (bathroom)?* Elicit the answer and show children how to draw a check in the living room column. Repeat with the other objects. When they're finished, ask: *Where does it go?* and they say where each item goes, e.g., *The shower goes in the bathroom*.

#  Look.  Circle. Say.

Concept

**Concept:** *in / on / under.* Ask: *What can you see?* Point to each picture in section 1, and ask: *Where's the teddy bear? (On / Under the table.)* Ask children which picture is different, and they circle it. Children identify and circle the different picture in each section. They then point to and describe each picture, saying where the teddy bear is.

 **Look.**  **Trace.**  **Say.**

Vocabulary

  sweep the floor

 cook

  make the bed

 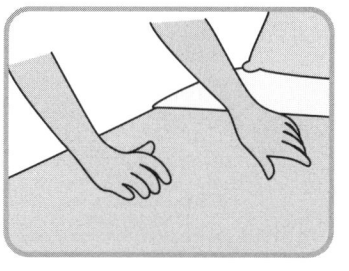 set the table

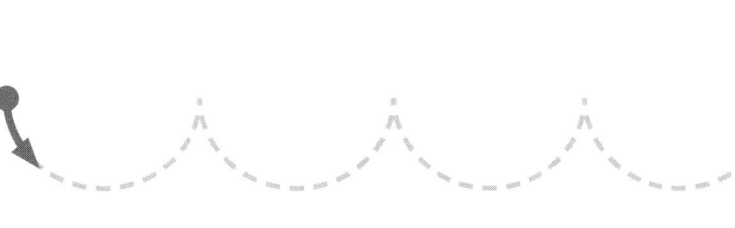  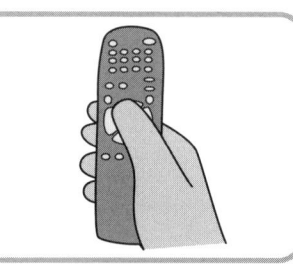 watch TV

**Vocabulary:** *set the table, sweep the floor, cook, watch TV, make the bed.* Children look at the pictures. Point to Leo and Mia's mom and ask: *What does she do at home?* Have children trace the line and say what she does at home: *She sweeps the floor.* Repeat for the other characters. Optional: Children trace the initial letter of each word / phrase.

Unit 3

 Look. Say. Circle.

Language

**Language:** *What's the (father) doing? He's / She's (cooking). The (father's cooking).* Children look at the two scenes. Then, they say what the people are doing in each scene, e.g., *Leo is making the bed*. Finally, children circle the differences in the second scene.

 **Look.**  **Say.**  **Match.**

**Speaking**

**Language:** *Where's (Mia)? He's / She's (in the kitchen). Where are you? I'm here! I'm (under the couch)!* Children name the two rooms at the top of the page. Explain that Leo and Mia are playing a hiding game. Point to the first small picture and ask: *Where's Mia? She's in the …?* Children look and match Mia to the corresponding hiding location in the scene above, saying: *She's in the kitchen.* Repeat with the other characters. Finally, children work in pairs, choose a hiding place in one of the scenes, and take turns asking and answering questions: *Where are you? I'm here. I'm (under the couch)!*

**Look.**  **Color.**  **Circle.** Say.

Cross-curricular: Social Studies

 =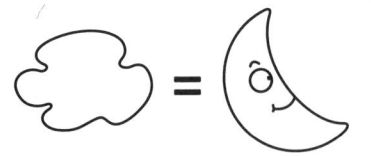

**Social Studies: Learning about daytime activities and nighttime activities.** Children choose two colors to represent *day* and *night*, and complete the key at the top of the page. They then circle each picture in the correct color according to their key. They point to each picture and describe it: *I (sleep) at night*.

 Trace. 1 2 3 Count. Color.

**Numeracy**

13   14   15

Numeracy: *thirteen, fourteen, fifteen.* Lead children in counting to 15. Point to 13 and the couches. Ask: *How many couches?* Point to the number 13, say the number, and have children repeat after you. Children trace 13. Then lead children in counting to 13. Say: *Let's count: one, two ... thirteen.* Children count and color only 13 couches. Repeat with 14 and 15.

Unit 3

Say.  Circle.  Draw.  Color.    Review

## What do we do at home?

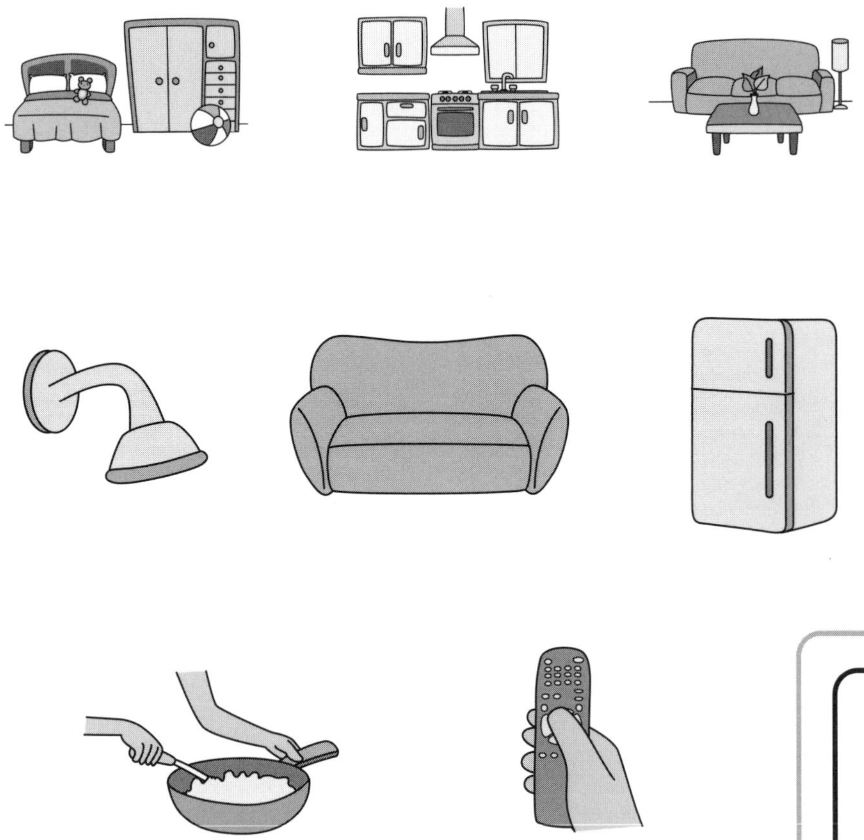

**My favorite thing in Unit 3:**

**Unit 3**

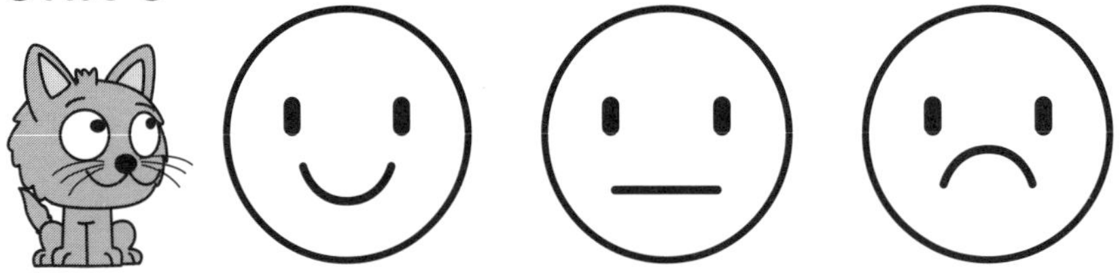

😊  😐  ☹

**Vocabulary and Language Review:** Ask the Big Question: *What do we do at home?* Children look back through Unit 3 to recall what they have learned. Ask them to look at the eight pictures from Unit 3. They say the words and then circle the pictures that they are able to name. Then ask: *What was your favorite thing in this unit?* Remind children of the song, story, cross-curricular lesson, etc. They draw a picture of their favorite thing. Children point to and talk about their pictures. Answer the Big Question together, using their pictures as a prompt. Finally, focus on the self-assessment activity. Ask: *How did you do in this unit?* Children color the face that shows how they feel they did.

# 4 What can we see on a farm?

 Point.  Stick.  Color. Say.

cow

horse

hen

sheep

duck

**Vocabulary:** *cow, hen, duck, horse, sheep.* Say each new word, and children point to each animal as you say it. Say: *(Cow / Hen)*. *Stick the (cow / hen)*. Children stick each sticker as you say it. Then name the other animals. Children color each animal as you say it. Finally, children point to and name each animal. Optional: Children trace the initial letter of each word, while repeating the word.

 Say.  Match.

Story

**Unit 4**

**Language: *What's missing? duck, hen, cat, sheep.*** Ask children to remember the story. Point to the first frame and ask: *What's missing? (The hen.)* They match the frame to the small picture of the hen. Repeat for the other frames. They should not match the duck to anything.

 **Look.**  **Say.**  **Circle.**  **Follow.**

**Phonics**

# Pp   Rr   Xx   Yy

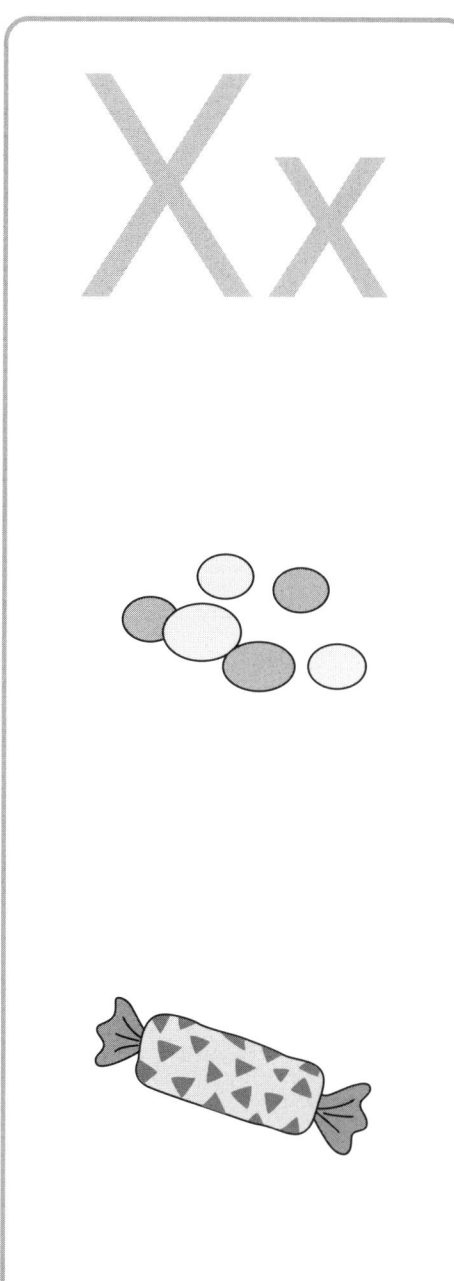
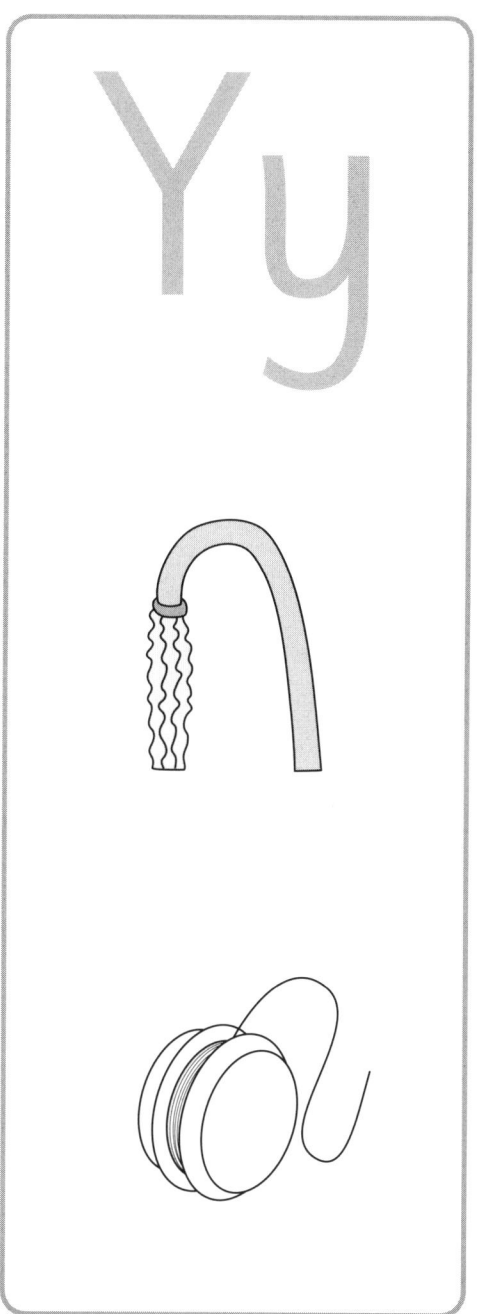

**Phonics:** *p*lant /p/, *r*abbit /r/, si*x* /ks/, *y*ellow /j/. Point to the first letter and say the sound /p/. Children repeat. Then point to each picture under it and say the word. Say: *P- p- Which word? (Plant.)* Show children how to circle the correct picture. Repeat with the other letters. Children circle the correct picture for each letter, then point and say the sounds and words. Point to the yo-yo and say: *A yellow yo-yo. Color the yo-yo yellow.* Then point to the rabbit and say: *A red rabbit. Color the rabbit red.* If your children have problems distinguishing between the *p* and *b* sounds, you could focus on the *bed*, and practice saying *plant* and *bed*. Finally, children follow the letters with their fingers. Optional: Children trace the letters with a pencil.

# Look. / Write. / Say. / Color.

**Literacy**

Do you like the story?

**Literacy: Identifying the sequence of a story.** Ask children to think about the story and remember what happens. Then focus on the four frames of the story. Children look carefully and number the frames in order. They then say what happens first / next / last, using the pictures as prompts. Finally, ask: *Do you like the story? (Yes. / No.)* Children color the happy face or the sad face.

👁 **Look.** 😃 **Say.** ✏ **Color.**

Values

**Values: Taking care of farm animals.** Children look at the scene. Point to the girl feeding the hens. Ask: *Is she taking care of something? (Yes.)* Then point to the boy playing with a ball and ask: *Is he taking care of something? (No.)* Discuss why not and what the boy could do better. Finally, children identify and color the people who are taking care of farm animals.

Unit 4  49

 **Look.**  **Point.**  **Match.**  **Say.**

Vocabulary

milk a cow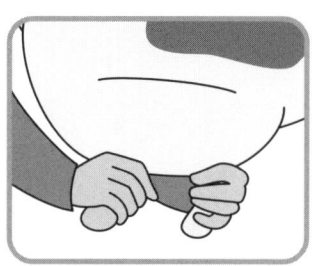

collect the eggs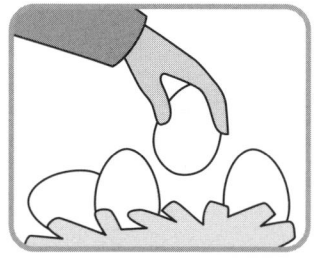

feed the ducks

shear a sheep

groom a horse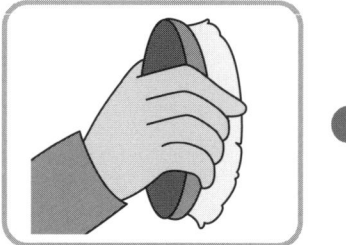

**Vocabulary:** *feed the ducks, milk a cow, groom a horse, shear a sheep, collect eggs.* Children point to the pictures in the first column and name each action. Then, they draw lines to match the actions on the left with the appropriate animal on the right. Finally, they finger trace the lines and say the phrases as they match the pictures. Optional: Children trace the initial letters of the phrases.

 Find. Match. Say.

Language

**Language: *What's the farmer doing? She's / He's (milking a cow).*** Point to the first farmer at the top. Ask: *What's she doing? (She's grooming a horse.)*
You could help children by pointing out the horse's ear on the puzzle piece. Children draw a line to match the two pieces. Repeat with the other puzzle pieces.
Then say a number between 1 and 5, and ask: *What's the farmer doing?* Children can take turns to say a number and ask a question for the class to answer.

Unit 4  51

 **Point. Say. Draw.**                                                Concept

**Concept: Recognizing patterns.** Children point to and name each animal. Then, they look at the sequence in each row and say what animal should come next. Guide them through the first row. Say: *Duck, cow, duck, cow, duck ... What comes next? (Cow.)* Children draw a cow in the empty space. If they struggle to draw the animals, they could color the cows brown, and the ducks yellow, then use color to complete the sequence. Continue with the other rows. Once children have finished drawing, ask them to repeat the completed sequences.

 Look.  Say.  Follow.

**Vocabulary**

duckling   lamb   foal   chick   calf

Vocabulary: *lamb, calf, chick, foal, duckling*. Children look at the adult animals at the top of the page and name them: *duck, hen, cow, sheep, horse*. Then, they follow the correct path with a crayon to the corresponding baby animal and say its name: *A baby (duck) is a (duckling)*. Optional: Children trace the initial letters of the words.

 Count. Write. Say.

Language

**Language:** *How many (cats) are there? There's one (cat). There are (two cows).* Children look at the animals in the barn and name each animal. Then, they count the animals in each section and write the correct number. Finally, children say: *There's one cat. There are (five ducks).*

 **Look.**  **Say.**  **Match.**

Speaking

**Language:** *What does a (cow) say? (Moo, moo!)* Children look at each picture at the top, and say the name of the animal. Ask: *What does a (cow) say?* and children make the animal noises. Focus on the first group of animals below. Name the three animals you can see, then ask: *What's missing?* Children draw lines to match the animals at the top of the page to the groups below. They then point and make the animal noises.

Unit 4

● Look. ✏ Color. ◯ Circle. ◡ Say.

Cross-curricular: Science

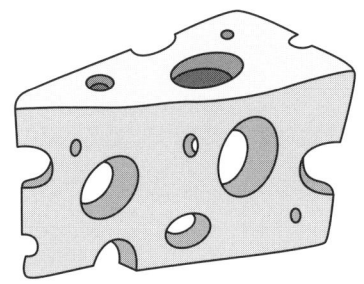

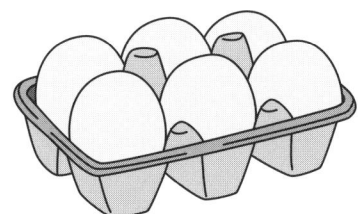

**Science: Learning what produce we get from farm animals.** Children choose three colors to represent *cow*, *sheep*, and *hen*, and complete the key at the top of the page. They then circle each picture in the correct color according to their key. Children do not need to circle all the pictures. They may also circle some pictures in two colors, e.g., cheese and milk can come from a cow or a sheep. They point to each picture and describe it: *(Milk) comes from a (cow).*

 **Trace.**  **Count.** **Color.**

**Numeracy**

16  17  18

**Numeracy:** *sixteen, seventeen, eighteen.* Lead children in counting to 18. Point to the hen and explain that this hen has left a lot of eggs! Ask: *How many eggs?* Point to the number 16, say the number, and have children repeat after you. Children trace 16. Then lead children in counting to 16. Say: *Let's count: one, two ... sixteen.* Children count and color only 16 eggs. Repeat with 17 and 18.

Unit 4 · 57

Say. Circle. Draw. Color.

Review

## What can we see on a farm?

**My favorite thing in Unit 4:**

**Unit 4**

**Vocabulary and Language Review:** Ask the Big Question: *What can we see on a farm?* Children look back through Unit 4 to recall what they have learned. Ask them to look at the eight pictures from Unit 4. They say the words and then circle the pictures that they are able to name. Accept all possible answers. Then ask: *What was your favorite thing in this unit?* Remind children of the song, story, cross-curricular lesson, etc. They draw a picture of their favorite thing. Children point to and talk about their pictures. Answer the Big Question together, using their pictures as a prompt. Finally, focus on the self-assessment activity. Ask: *How did you do in this unit?* Children color the face that shows how they feel they did.

# 5 What meals do we eat?

 Point.   Stick.   Color.  Say.

## breakfast

## lunch

## dinner

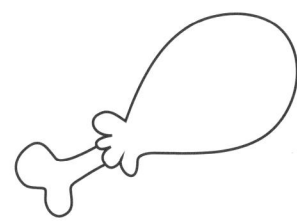
## chicken

## eggs

## salad

**Vocabulary: breakfast, lunch, dinner, eggs, chicken, salad.** Say each new word, and children point to each item as you say it. Say: *(Breakfast / Salad). Stick the (breakfast / salad).* Children stick each sticker as you say it. Then name the other items. Children color each item as you say it. They then point to and name each item. Finally, children can trace the words.

 Say. Draw.

Story

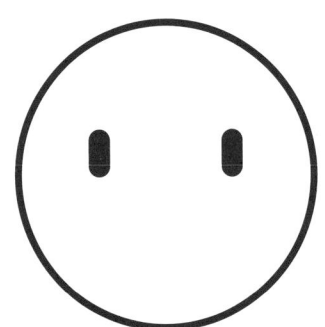
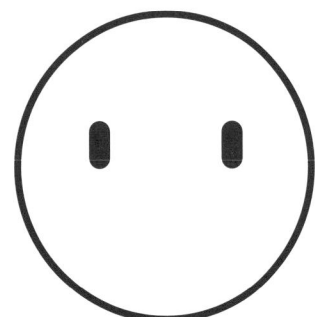
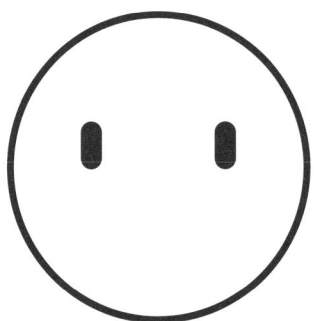

**Language:** *Is Pat (happy)? happy, sad.* Ask children to remember the story. Point to each picture. Ask: *Is Pat happy or sad?* Children answer: *She's happy / sad.* They draw the mouth on each emoji according to how she feels.

 **Look.**  **Say.**  **Match.**  **Trace.**

**Phonics**

Pat

sad

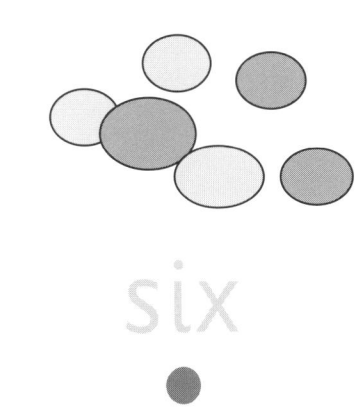
six

Aa

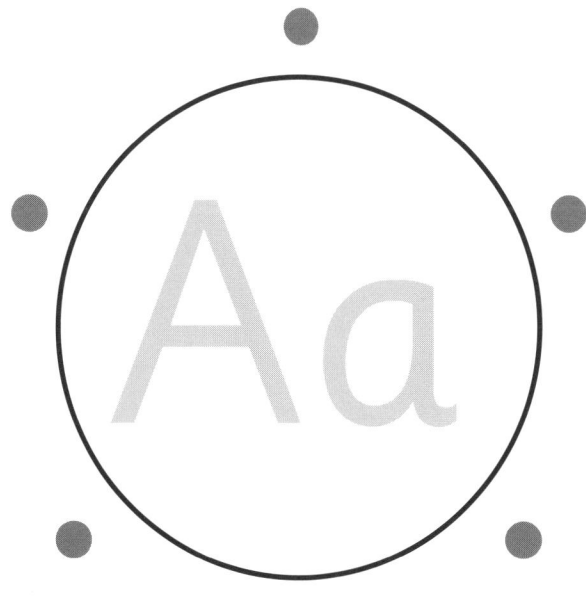

Dad

sun

**Phonics:** *Pat, sad, Dad* /æ/. Point to the letters in the middle and say the sound /æ/. Children repeat. Then point to the first picture (*Pat*), and say: A - a - a - Pat? (Yes.) Show children how to draw a line from the picture to the letters in the middle because it has the /æ/ sound. Repeat with the other pictures. Children draw lines from the pictures with the /æ/ sound to the letters Aa in the middle. Children point to these pictures and say the words. Finally, they follow the letters of the words with their finger, then trace the letters and the words with a pencil.

 Look. Match. Say. Color.  Literacy

1.
2.
3.
4.

Do you like the story?

# ✏️ Draw. 👄 Say.

**Values**

**Values: Eating a healthy breakfast.** Ask: *What do you eat for breakfast?* Children draw themselves eating breakfast. They draw the food and drink that they have. Then they point and say: *I eat a healthy breakfast!*

Unit 5

 Look.  Match.  Say.

**Vocabulary**

water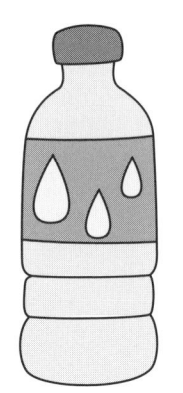

pancakes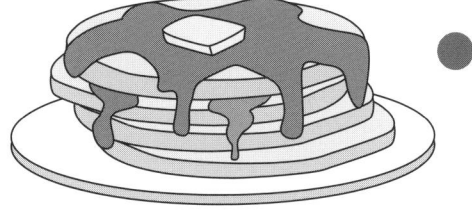

soup

rice

**Vocabulary:** *water, pancakes, soup, rice.* Children look at each picture on the left and name each food. Focus on the first group of foods on the right. Name the three foods you can see, then ask: *What's missing?* Children draw lines to match the foods on the left to the groups on the right. They then point and name each food. Finally, children can trace the words.

 Match.  Say.  Think.

Language

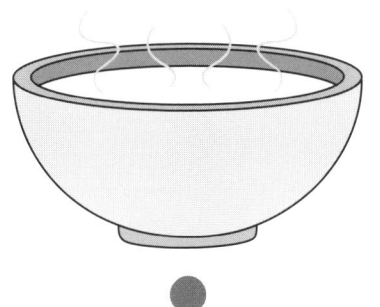 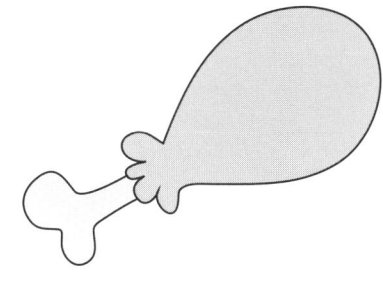 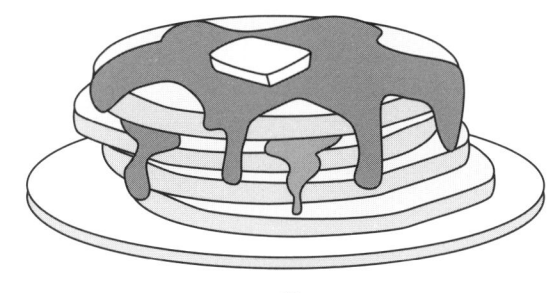 

   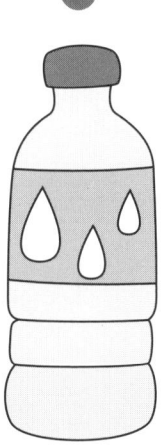

**Language:** *What food do you like? I like (soup). I don't like (cheese).* Point to the food pictures and children say the words. Point to one food and say: *Mmm! I like (chicken)!* With your finger draw a line from the food to the happy face. Repeat with another food and *don't like*. Children look at all the foods, think about whether they like them, and draw lines to match them to the right face for them. Ask a child: *What food do you like?* They point to different foods in their book and say: *I like (soup). I don't like (apples).* Then ask the class: *What does (Alex) like?* They try to remember, and say: *He (likes) (rice).*

Unit 5

 Look. Say. Draw.

Concept

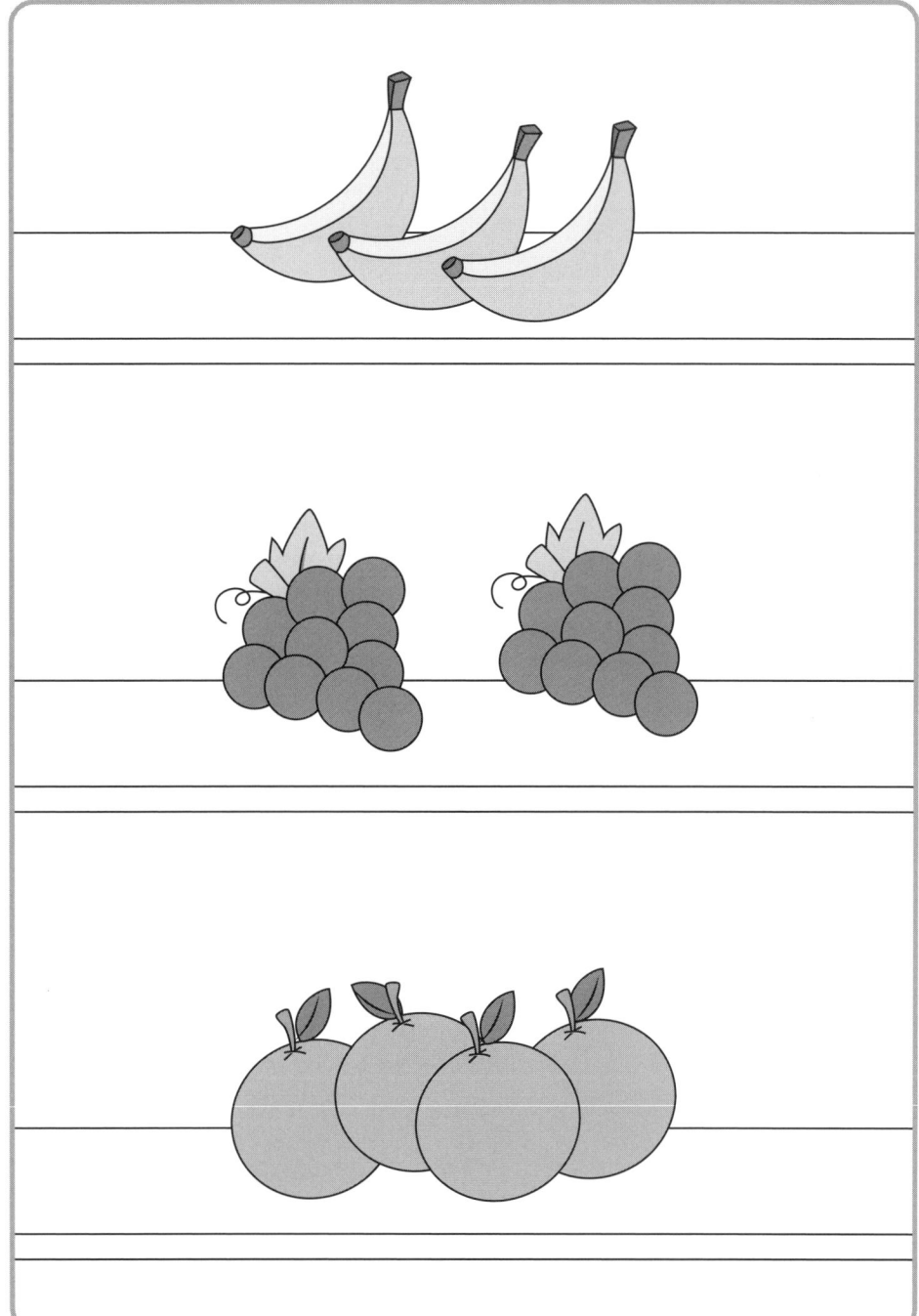
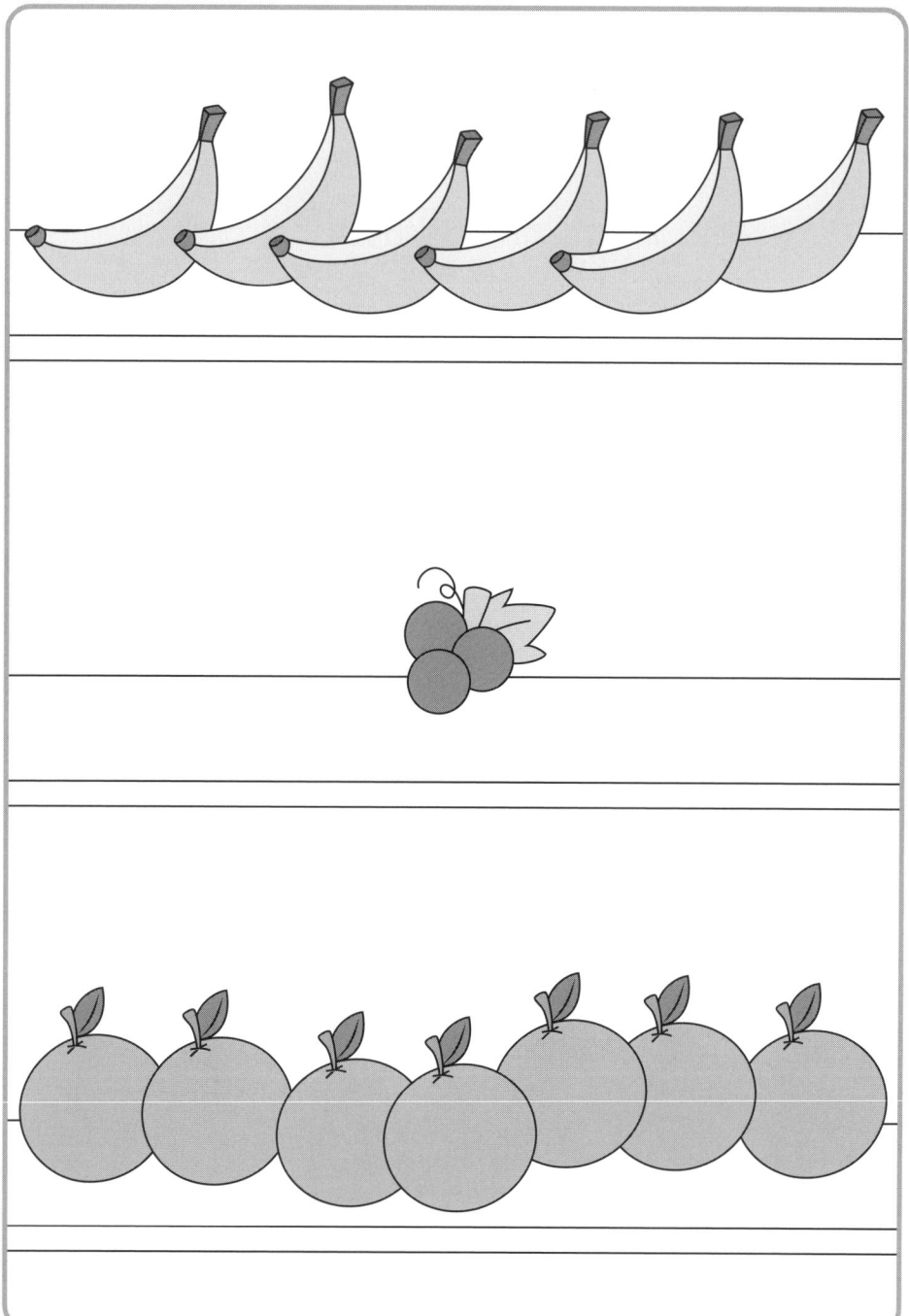

**Concept: *a few / a lot*.** Children look at the two scenes. Then they say how many of each food they can see in each scene, e.g., *A few bananas. A lot of bananas.* Finally, children draw what's missing in the scene with the fewer fruits so both scenes have a lot of fruits. (They don't have to draw the exact number of the missing fruits in each scene.)

 Say. ✓ Check.

**Vocabulary**

|  |  ☀ (sunrise) | ☀ (sun) | 🌙 (moon) |
|---|---|---|---|
| milk |  |  |  |
| orange juice |  |  |  |
| cereal |  |  |  |
| fish |  |  |  |
| strawberries |  |  |  |

**Vocabulary:** *milk, orange juice, cereal, fish, strawberries.* Point to the three pictures across the top and explain that they show different times of day when we eat our meals. Elicit which represents *breakfast, lunch,* and *dinner.* Children look at the food and drinks and name each. They then think about when they eat or drink that item and put checks in the spaces accordingly. Point out that they can check more than one space if, for example, they drink milk at breakfast and also at dinner. Finally, children can trace the words.

 Color. Draw. Say.

**Language**

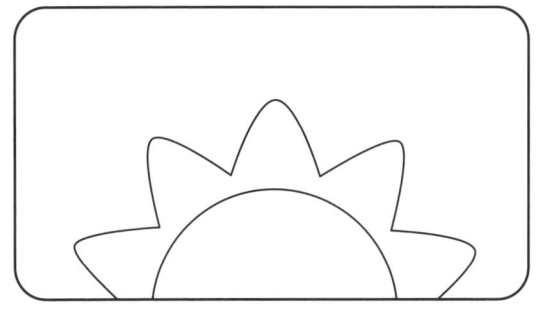

**Language:** *What do you have for (breakfast)? I have (eggs) for breakfast. We have (breakfast) in the (morning).* Point to the pictures at the top of each box and discuss what times of day they represent and what meal we eat at each time. Then ask: *What do you have for breakfast?* Children color the pictures that represent times of day and draw what they eat and drink at each time. Finally, they describe their meals: *I have (breakfast) in the (morning). I have (eggs) for (breakfast).*

# Look. Say. Color.

**Speaking**

**Language:** *What do you want for (breakfast)? (Milk), please.* **Point to Leo's thought bubble and ask:** *Breakfast or lunch? (Breakfast.)* Ask what food children can see. Then ask: *Leo, what do you want for breakfast?* and children repeat. Say: *Milk and pancakes, please.* Children repeat. Repeat with Mia and lunch. Divide the class into two groups, and tell one group they are Leo and the other group they are Mia. Point to Leo, and have the Mia group ask: *What do you want for breakfast?* The Leo group answers. Repeat with the other picture. Repeat several times with large and small groups of children. You could invite confident children to come to the front and act Leo or Mia with you as the other character. Finally, children can color the meal that they would like to eat.

Unit 5 69

## Look. Color. Circle. Say.

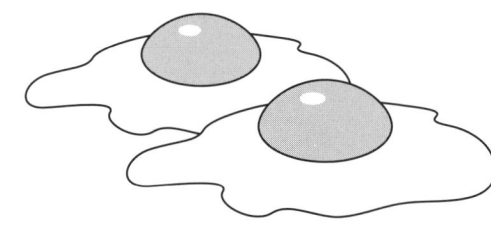

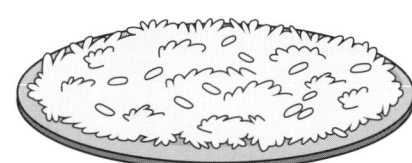
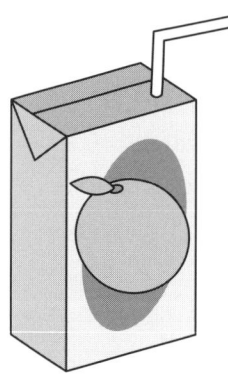
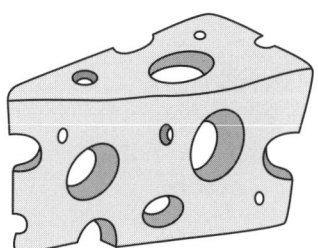

**Cross-curricular: Science**

**Science: Learning which food comes from plants.** Children choose two colors to represent *animals* and *plants*, and complete the key at the top of the page. They then circle each picture in the correct color according to their key. They point to each picture and describe it: *(Strawberries) come from (plants).*

 Trace.  Count.  Match. ✏️ Color.

**Numeracy**

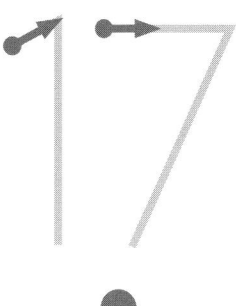  

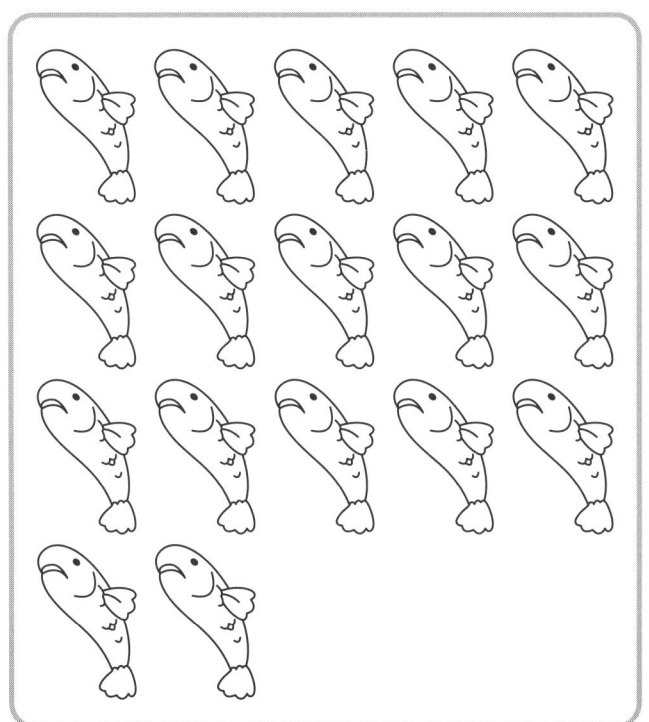  

**Numeracy:** *nineteen.* Lead children in counting to 19. They trace the numbers 17, 18, and 19. Point to the fish and say: *How many fish? Let's count!* Repeat with the other foods. Children match the numbers to the foods. Finally, they can color the foods.

Unit 5 — 71

 Say. Circle. Draw. Color.

Review

## What meals do we eat?

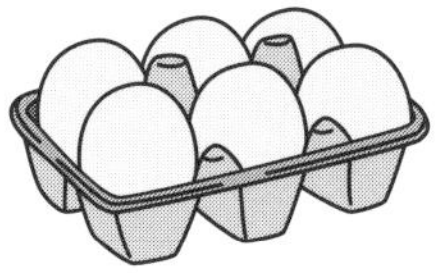

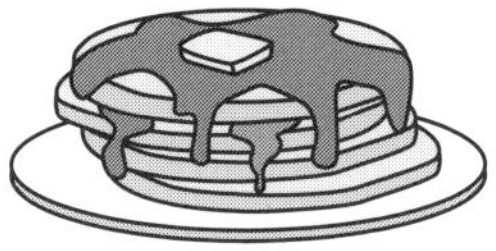

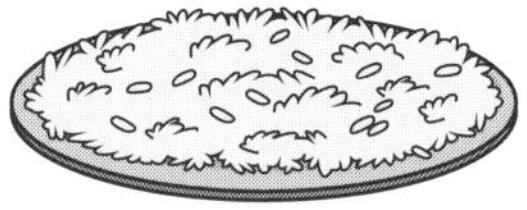

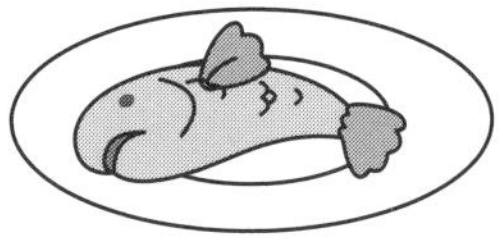

**My favorite thing in Unit 5:**

**Unit 5**

**Vocabulary and Language Review:** Ask the Big Question: *What meals do we eat?* Children look back through Unit 5 to recall what they have learned. Ask them to look at the eight pictures from Unit 5. They say the words and then circle the pictures that they are able to name. Then ask: *What was your favorite thing in this unit?* Remind children of the song, story, cross-curricular lesson, etc. They draw a picture of their favorite thing. Children point to and talk about their pictures. Answer the Big Question together, using their pictures as a prompt. Finally, focus on the self-assessment activity. Ask: *How did you do in this unit?* Children color the face that shows how they feel they did.

# 6 What clothes do we wear?

 Point.  Stick.  Color.  Say.

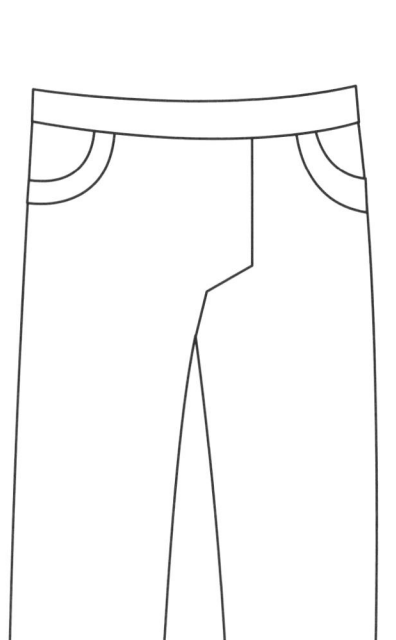

shoes

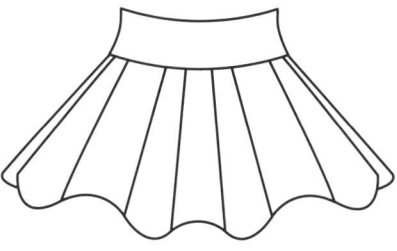
skirt

pants

T-shirt

sweater

**Vocabulary:** *pants, shoes, T-shirt, skirt, sweater.* Say each new word, and children point to each item as you say it. Say: *(Shoes / T-shirt).* Stick the *(shoes / T-shirt).* Children stick each sticker as you say it. Then name the other items. Children color each item as you say it. They then point to and name each item. Finally, children can trace the words.

 Match. Say.  Story

**Language:** *Which teddy bear is missing? What is this teddy bear wearing? It's wearing (a scarf). scarf, wig, tie, shoes, cape, teddy bear.* Ask children to remember the story. Point to the first frame and ask: *Which teddy bear is missing?* Children draw a line to match the missing teddy bear to the picture. Repeat with the other pictures. Point to each teddy bear and ask: *What is this teddy bear wearing?* Children answer: *It's wearing (a tie).* Encourage them to say the colors from the story too if they remember, e.g., *It's wearing a pink tie.*

#  Look.  Say.  Match.  Trace.

**Phonics**

wig

fish

big

Dad

Ii

milk

**Phonics:** *wig, big, pink* /ɪ/. Point to the letters Ii in the middle and say the sound /ɪ/. Children repeat. Then point to the first picture *(wig)*, and say: *I - i - i - Wig. Show me i*. Children point to the *i* in the word *wig*. Children draw a line to match the picture to the letters in the middle. Children look at all the pictures and words, and draw lines to match the ones with the /ɪ/ sound to the letters in the middle. They can also underline the *i* in each word. Finally, they follow the letters of the words with their finger, then trace the letters and the words with a pencil.

Unit 6 75

# Look. Color. Say.

Literacy

## Do you like the story? 🙂 ☹️

**Literacy: Identifying details from a story.** Ask the class to look at the teddy bears from the story. Ask: *Can you remember? What are they wearing?* Elicit ideas and check if necessary. Children color the clothing items to match the characters in the story. Finally, ask: *Do you like the story? (Yes. / No.)* Children color the happy face or the sad face.

# 👁 Look. 😀 Say. ✏️ Color.

Values

**Values: Taking care of our clothes.** Point to the girl hanging up her jacket. Ask: *What's she doing? (Taking care of her clothes.)* Then point to the boy throwing his jacket on the floor and ask: *Is he taking care of his clothes? (No.)* Discuss why not and what the child could do better. Finally, children identify and color the children who are taking care of their clothes.

Unit 6

Say. Count. Write.

Vocabulary

socks     jacket     raincoat     boots     dress

**Vocabulary:** *socks, jacket, boots, raincoat, dress.* Children look at the pictures at the top of the page and name each item. Then, they search for each item in the box and count them. You may need to explain in L1 that each pair of socks and boots counts as one, i.e., there are three (pairs of) socks and three (pairs of) boots. Finally, say together: *How many (jackets)? (Three! Three jackets!)* Children write the number next to each item. Finally, children can trace the words.

Unit 6

 Color. Say.

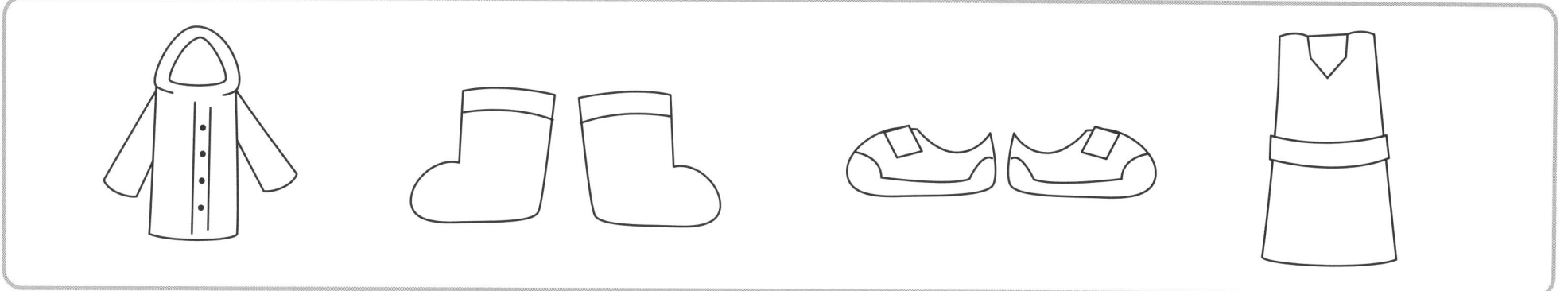

**Language:** *What color is the (raincoat)? What color are the (shoes)? What's he / she wearing? He's / She's wearing (a yellow raincoat and red boots).* Point to each item of clothing across the top as children name them. Then distribute crayons and ask children to color each item in a different color. Children work in pairs and take turns asking: *What color is the (dress)? What color are the (shoes)? The (dress) is (purple). The (shoes) are (black).* They color the children's clothes according to their partner's key. Finally, they share their coloring and take turns describing the children, saying: *He's / She's wearing (a purple dress and black shoes).*

 Look. Color. Say.

Concept

◯ = ✋ left

◯ = ✋ right

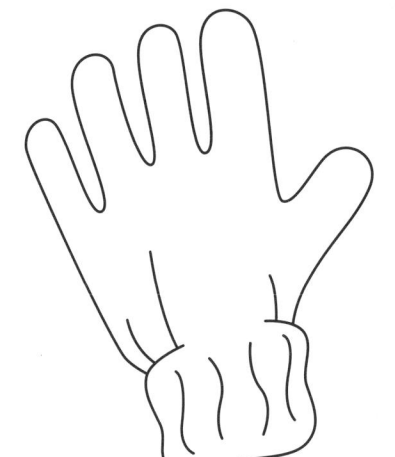
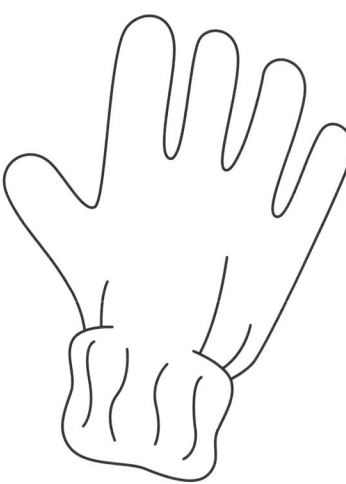

**Concept: *left*, *right*.** Look at the items of clothing and point out that each pair has a left and a right. Children choose two colors to represent *left* and *right*, and complete the key at the top of the page. They then color the left and right item in each pair in the correct color according to their key. They point to each picture and describe it: *(Boots!) Left, right.*

 Say. ✓ Check.

Vocabulary

sunny

snowy

cloudy

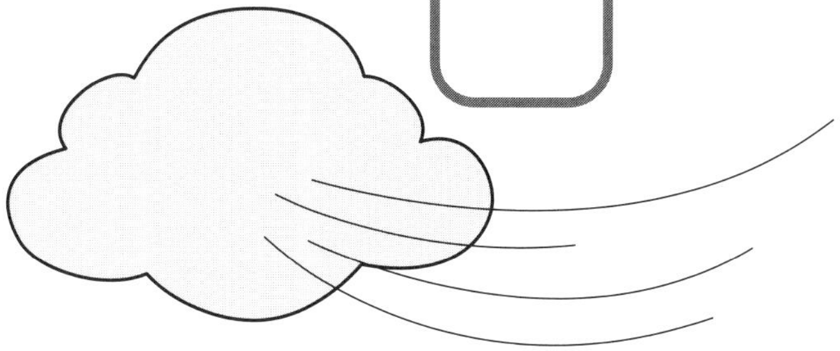

windy

rainy

**Vocabulary:** *sunny, snowy, cloudy, windy, rainy.* If possible, take the children outside, or gather them by a window, to look at the weather today. Ask: *What's the weather like?* Make sure they understand that we can often use more than one word to describe the weather. It could be *cloudy, windy,* and *rainy*. On the page, point to each picture, and children say the word. They then check the pictures that describe the weather today. Finally, children can trace the words and say them aloud.

Unit 6  81

 **Look. Circle. Say.** — Language

**Language:** *What's the weather like today? It's (sunny). What's (Mia / Leo) wearing? She's / He's wearing (a dress) and (shoes).* Point to each weather picture and ask: *What's the weather like today? (It's snowy / sunny / rainy.)* Then point to the characters and ask: *What's (Mia) wearing?* Explain that children should circle the character wearing the appropriate clothes for the weather. Finally, children say what the weather is like and what each appropriately dressed child is wearing: *It's (snowy). (Leo) is wearing (a jacket) and (boots).*

# Look. Say. Draw.

Speaking

**Language:** *What's the weather like today? It's (rainy). Put on your (raincoat)!* Point to each picture and ask: *What's the weather like?* Children respond: *It's rainy. It's snowy / cold.* Point to Mia and ask: *What can we say to Mia? Put on your raincoat!* Children repeat. They draw Mia's raincoat. Repeat with Leo and his hat and boots. Divide the class into two groups, and tell one group they are Mia and the other group they are Leo. Point to Mia and have the Mia group say: *It's rainy.* The Leo group answers: *Put on your raincoat!* Repeat with the other picture. Repeat several times with large and small groups of children. You could invite confident children to come to the front and act Leo or Mia with you as the other character.

Unit 6

# 👁 Look. ✏️ Draw. 👄 Say.

**Cross-curricular: Science**

**Science: Learning about the four seasons.** Point to the flower, and ask children to name the season. *(Spring.)* Ask them what things they do in spring. Repeat with the other seasons. Children draw themselves doing something they enjoy doing in each season. Finally, they point to each season and say what they enjoy doing.

Trace.  Count.  Match. Color.  Numeracy

15   18   20

 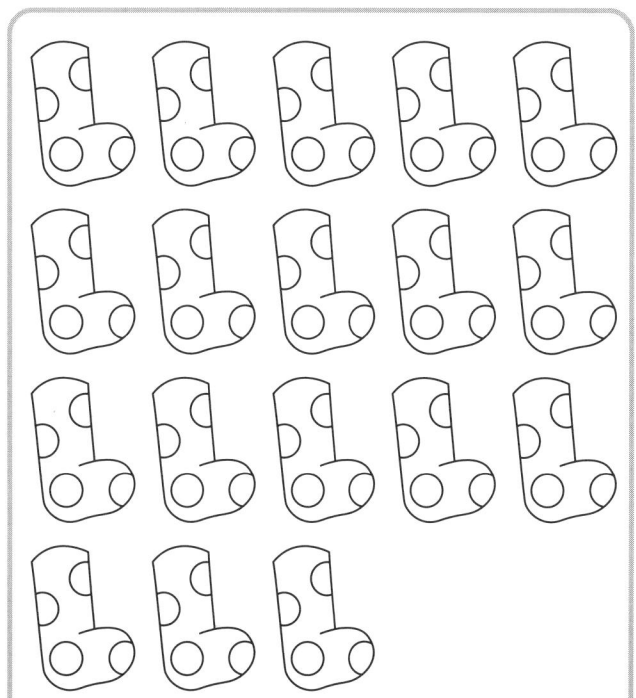 

**Numeracy: *twenty*.** Lead children in counting to 20. They trace the numbers 15, 18, and 20. Point to the T-shirts and say: *How many T-shirts? Let's count!* Repeat with the other clothes. Children match the numbers to the clothes. Finally, they can color the clothes in colors of their preference.

Say. Circle. Draw. Color.   Review

**My favorite thing in Unit 6:**

**Unit 6**

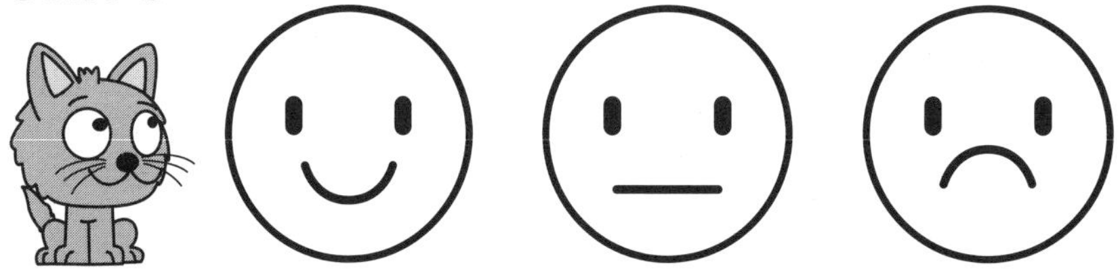

**Vocabulary and Language Review:** Ask the Big Question: *What clothes do we wear?* Children look back through Unit 6 to recall what they have learned. Ask them to look at the eight pictures from Unit 6. They say the words and then circle the pictures that they are able to name. Then ask: *What was your favorite thing in this unit?* Remind children of the song, story, cross-curricular lesson, etc. They draw a picture of their favorite thing. Children point to and talk about their pictures. Answer the Big Question together, using their pictures as a prompt. Finally, focus on the self-assessment activity. Ask: *How did you do in this unit?* Children color the face that shows how they feel they did.

# 7 What can we do with our senses?

 Point.    Stick.    Color.    Say.

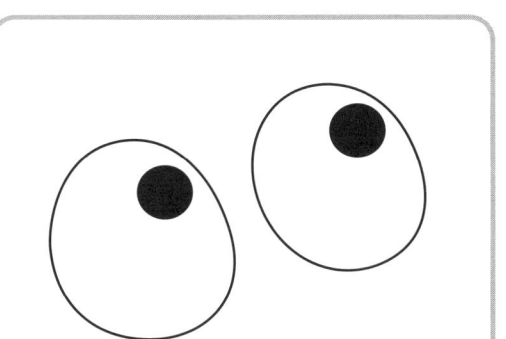
see

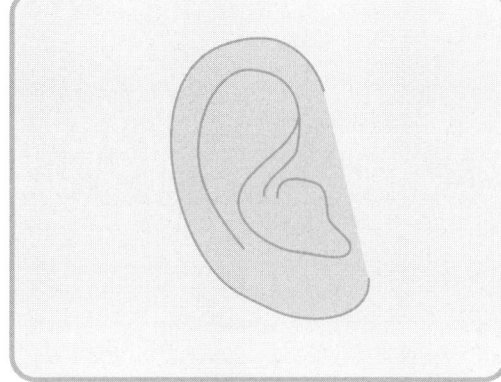
hear

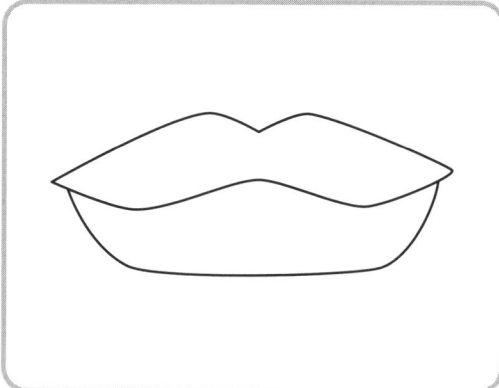
taste

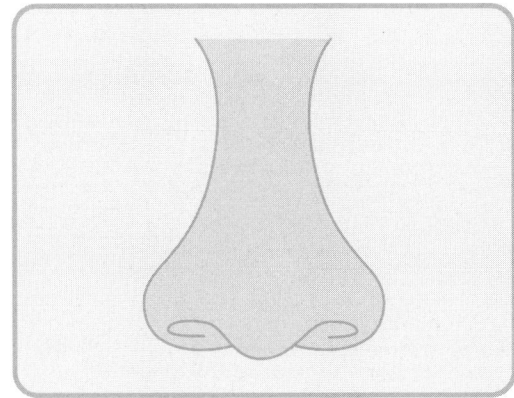
smell

touch

**Vocabulary:** *see, touch, hear, smell, taste.* Say each new word, and children point to each action as you say it. Say: *(Hear / Smell). Stick (hear / smell).* Children stick each sticker as you say it. Then name the other actions. Children color each action as you say it. They then point to and name each action. Finally, children can trace the words.

Unit 7   87

 Look. Circle. Color.

Story

**Language:** *What can you see? apple pie.* Ask children to remember the story. They look at the pictures and circle five differences between them. (In the first picture, there aren't any apples, there are two birds, the boy is happy, the dad isn't smiling, the mom is holding something.) They then color the circle of the picture that is from the story.

Unit 7

 **Look.** **Say.** **Trace.**

Phonics

# Uu

sun

sing

Gus

bug

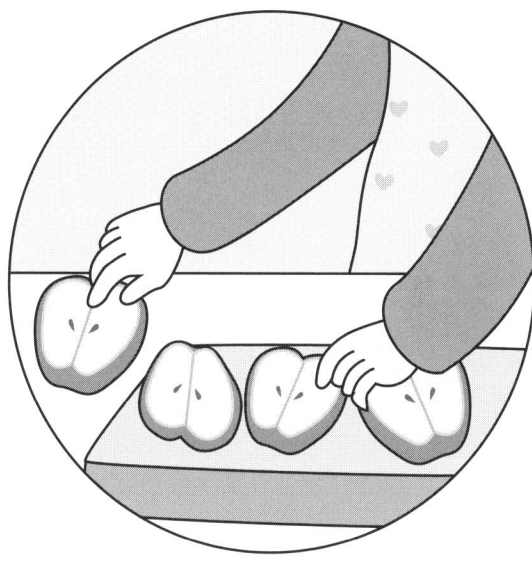

cut

cat

**Phonics:** *sun*, *Gus*, *cut* /ʌ/. Point to the letters at the top of the page and say the sound /ʌ/. Point to the first picture and children say the word. (*Sun.*) Then point to the two words under it, and help children sound them out. Ask: *Which word is sun?* Children point to the correct word. Repeat with the other pictures and words. Children point to and say the words. Finally, they follow the letters of the words with their finger, then trace the letters and the words with a pencil.

Unit 7  89

# 👁 Look. 👄 Say. ✏️ Color.

Literacy

**Do you like the story?**

**Literacy: Identifying details from a story.** Children look at the scenes. Point to each scene and ask: *Is this scene from the story? (Yes. / No.)* Children color the frames of the scenes from the story. Finally, ask: *Do you like the story? (Yes. / No.)* Children color the happy face or the sad face.

# Think. Circle. Draw.

**Values**

**Values: Respecting differences and recognizing similarities.** Remind children that there are lots of different ways to enjoy a story. Point to the two pictures at the top of the page and ask children to circle their favorite way to enjoy a story. Encourage children to share their ideas, and to listen to others' ideas. Remind children that everyone enjoys different things, and that's OK. Then ask children to think about their favorite story. Finally, children draw a picture of their favorite story inside the empty book. They can show their pictures to the class.

 Say. Color.

**Vocabulary**

| | good | |
| | bad | |
| | soft | |
| | rough | |
| | smooth | |

**Vocabulary:** *soft, rough, smooth, good, bad.* Point to the picture of the nose, sniff a little, and ask: *How does it smell?* Point to the *good* picture and children answer: *Good!* Children color only the picture(s) in the row that smell good. Repeat with *bad*. Then continue, pointing to the hand and the *soft* picture, and asking: *How does it feel?* Again children color the representative pictures. Finally, children can trace the words.

 **Think. Draw. Say.**  Language

**Language:** *How does it smell? It smells (good). How does it feel? It feels (soft).* Point to Mia, and say: *It smells good!* Ask: *What things smell good?* Accept all children's opinions and ideas. Children draw something that they think smells good. Repeat with Leo, saying: *It feels soft. What things feel soft?* Children point to their pictures and describe them: *(She's) (smelling) a (flower). How does it (smell)? It (smells) (good).*

Unit 7

**Concept:** *between / next to / behind.* Name an object in the scene. Children look for the object in the picture, point to the object, and name it. Repeat with all objects. Then ask about the position of random objects: *Where is (Tickles)?* Children respond using the language: *(Tickles) is (behind the table).* Point to the pencil at the top of the page and say: *The pencil is between the couch and the TV.* Children draw the pencil in the correct place in the scene. Repeat with the other two objects, saying: *The ball is behind the couch. The apple is next to Tickles.* Once children finish drawing the objects, ask them to show their pictures, and ask: *Where's the (ball)?* Children respond.

👁 Look.  ✏ Color.  ◯ Circle.  👄 Say.

Vocabulary

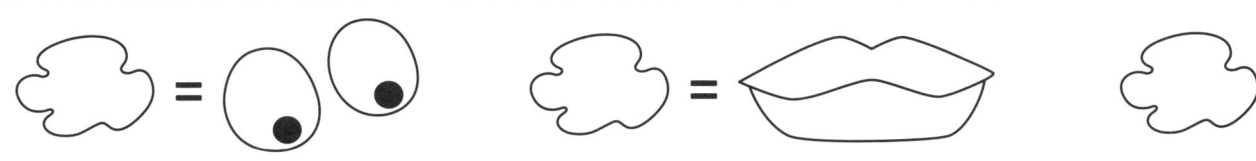

loud

salty

sweet

beautiful

quiet

**Vocabulary:** *sweet, salty, loud, quiet, beautiful.* Children choose three colors to represent *see, taste,* and *hear,* and complete the key at the top of the page. They then circle each picture in the correct color according to their key. They point to each picture and say: *It (looks) (beautiful).* Finally, children can trace the words.

Unit 7  95

 Trace. Say.

Language

**Language:** *How does it (sound)? It (sounds loud).* Children trace the line from each sense or body part to the object at the bottom of the page. Point to each picture and matching body part. Children ask the appropriate question: *How does it (sound)?* Finally, children describe the object: *It (sounds loud).*

 **Look. Match. Say.**

Speaking

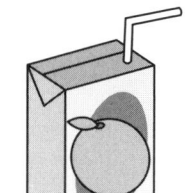
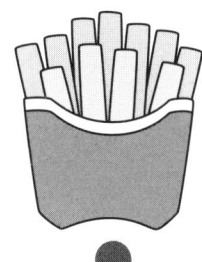

It tastes sweet.

It tastes salty.

**Language:** *How does it taste? It tastes (sweet).* Point to the lollipop in Mia's speech bubble, saying: *It tastes sweet.* Repeat with the popcorn in Leo's speech bubble, saying: *It tastes salty.* Then point to the pineapple and ask: *How does it taste? (It tastes sweet.)* Demonstrate drawing a line from the pineapple to Mia. Repeat with the pizza. Children match all the foods to Mia and Leo. Finally, they point to each food item and say: *It tastes (salty / sweet).*

Unit 7

 Look. Say. Check.

**Cross-curricular: Science**

**Science: Exploring our senses.** Point to each body part in the first column and ask: *Which sense is it?* Children name the five senses. Children look at the first picture in the top row (the guitar). Ask: *Can you see / hear / smell / taste / touch a guitar?* Children check the section next to the senses we use to perceive a guitar. Repeat with the other pictures. Finally, children say how they can perceive each item, e.g., *I can see a guitar. I can hear a train.*

¹²₃ Count. ✏️ Trace.

**Numeracy**

20

10

30

**Numeracy: thirty.** Ask: *How many fingers on the hands?* Point to the first pair of hands and say: *Let's count!* Count to 10 together. Continue with the other pairs of hands. Children trace the fingers on the last pair of hands. Then say: *How many sets of ten? (Three.) How many fingers? Let's count by tens: Ten, twenty, thirty!* Children trace and say the numbers.

Unit 7

Say. Circle. Draw. Color.

Review

## What can we do with our senses?

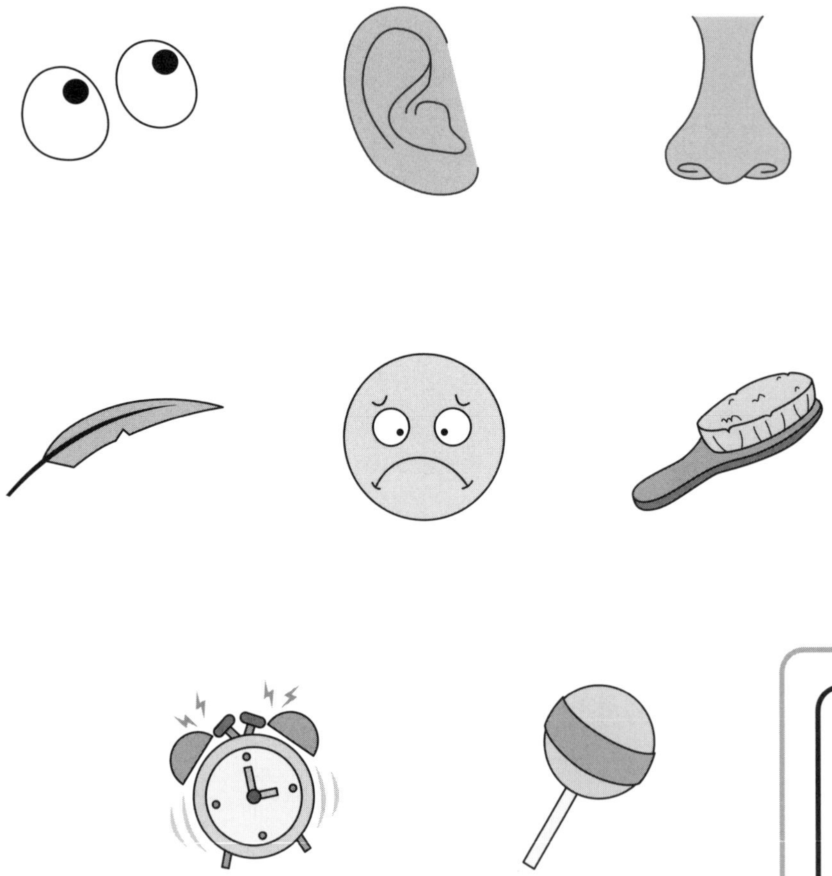

**My favorite thing in Unit 7:**

**Unit 7**

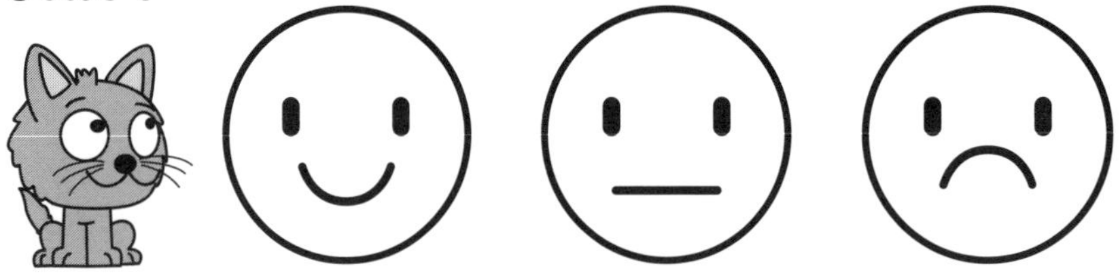

**Vocabulary and Language Review:** Ask the Big Question: *What can we do with our senses?* Children look back through Unit 7 to recall what they have learned. Ask them to look at the eight pictures from Unit 7. They say the words and then circle the pictures that they are able to name. Accept all possible answers. Then ask: *What was your favorite thing in this unit?* Remind children of the song, story, cross-curricular lesson, etc. They draw a picture of their favorite thing. Children point to and talk about their pictures. Answer the Big Question together, using their pictures as a prompt. Finally, focus on the self-assessment activity. Ask: *How did you do in this unit?* Children color the face that shows how they feel they did.

 # How do we travel?

 Point.  Stick.  Color.  Say.

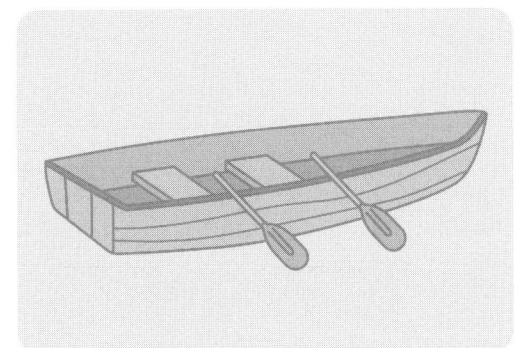
boat

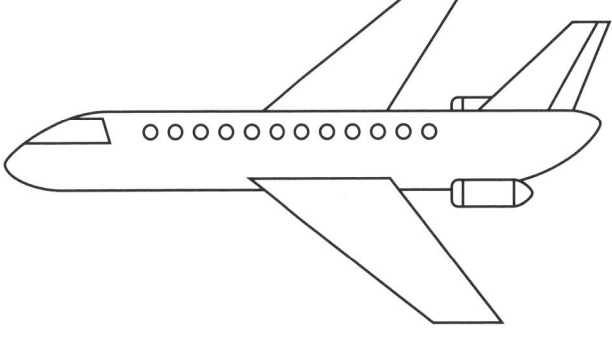
airplane

car

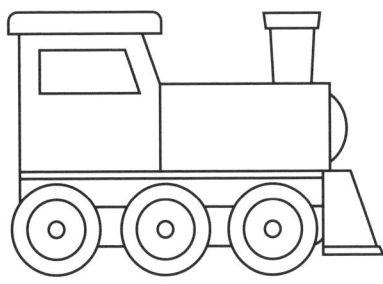
train

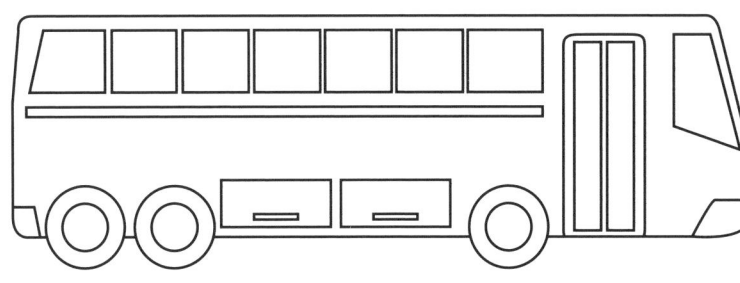
bus

**Vocabulary:** *car, train, bus, airplane, boat.* Say each new word, and children point to each item as you say it. Say: *(Boat / Car). Stick the (boat / car).* Children stick each sticker as you say it. Then name the other items. Children color each item as you say it. They then point to and name each item. Finally, children can trace the words.

 Say. ✓ Check.

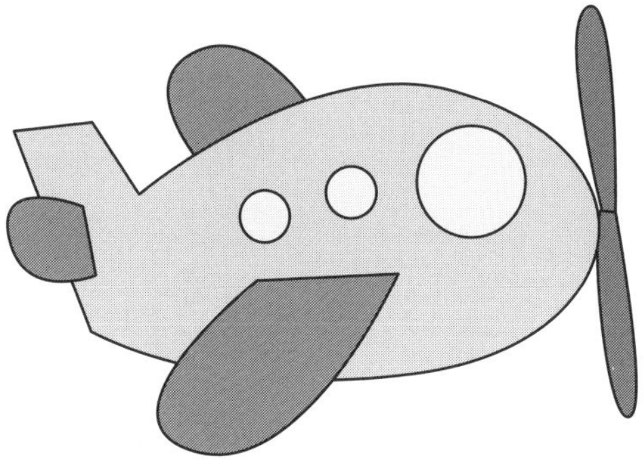

Story

**Language:** *Is there a (train)? Yes, there is. No, there isn't. train, bus, car, boat, airplane.* Ask children to remember the story. Point to each form of transportation. Ask: *Is there a (train)?* Children answer *Yes, there is.* or *No, there isn't.* They check the transportation that is in the story (train, bus, airplane).

Unit 8

 Look.  Match.  Say.  Trace.

 Phonics

Oo

tap

top

bib

Bob

pop

**Phonics:** *top*, *Bob* /ɒ/. Point to the letters between the two pictures and say the sound /ɒ/. Point to the first picture and children say the word (*top*). Then point to the word *tap*, and help children sound it out. Say: *T - a - p. Tap. Is this top? (No.)* Repeat with other words until children find the correct word. They draw a line to match the word to the picture. Repeat with the other picture. Children point to and say the words. Finally, they follow the letters of the words with their finger, then trace the letters and the words with a pencil.

Unit 8  103

 Say. Circle. Color.

Literacy

Do you like the story?

#  Look. Say. Color.

**Values**

**Values: Caring for the environment.** Focus on the pictures. Point to each one and ask: *Is this good for the environment?* Help children to understand that all of these can be good for the environment. Point to the first picture and say: *Walk. Do you sometimes walk places?* Children raise their hands if they sometimes do this. Repeat with the other pictures. Children color the frames of the pictures that show what they sometimes do.

Unit 8 105

 Say. Trace. Color.

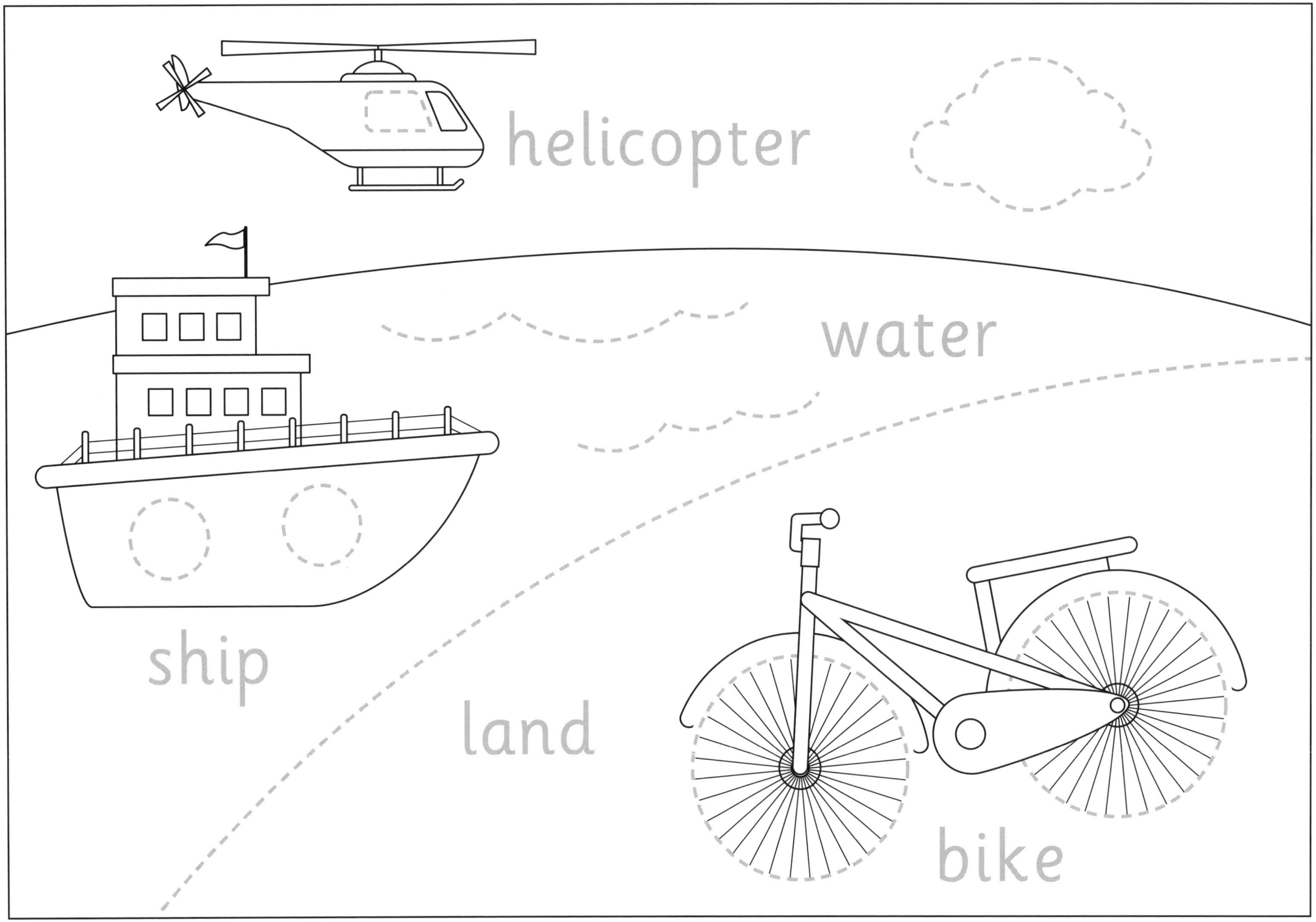

Vocabulary

helicopter

water

ship

land

bike

 **Language**

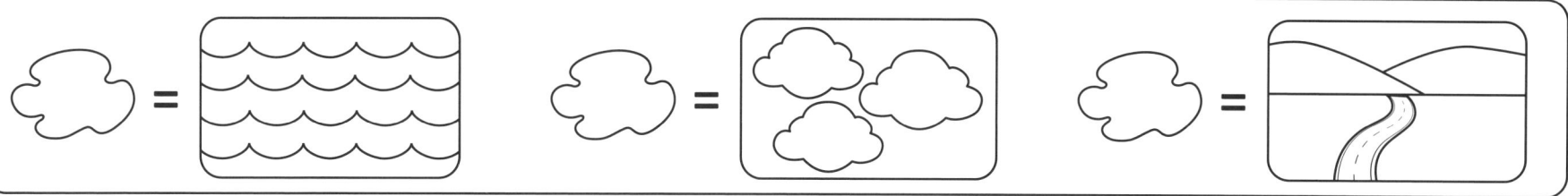

 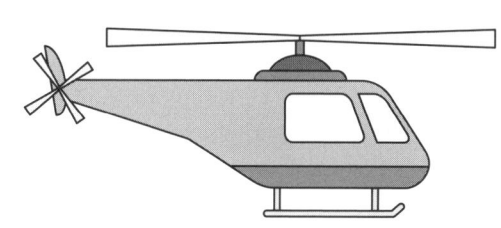 

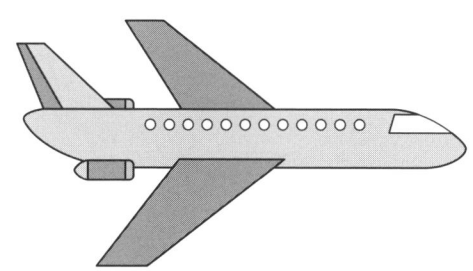 

**Language:** *Where does (an airplane) go? (An airplane) goes (in the air).* Children choose three colors to represent *water*, *air*, and *land*, and complete the key at the top of the page. They then circle each picture in the correct color according to their key. They point to each picture and describe it: *(A car) goes (on land).*

Unit 8 107

👁 Look.  ⭯ Circle.  ⌣ Say.

Concept

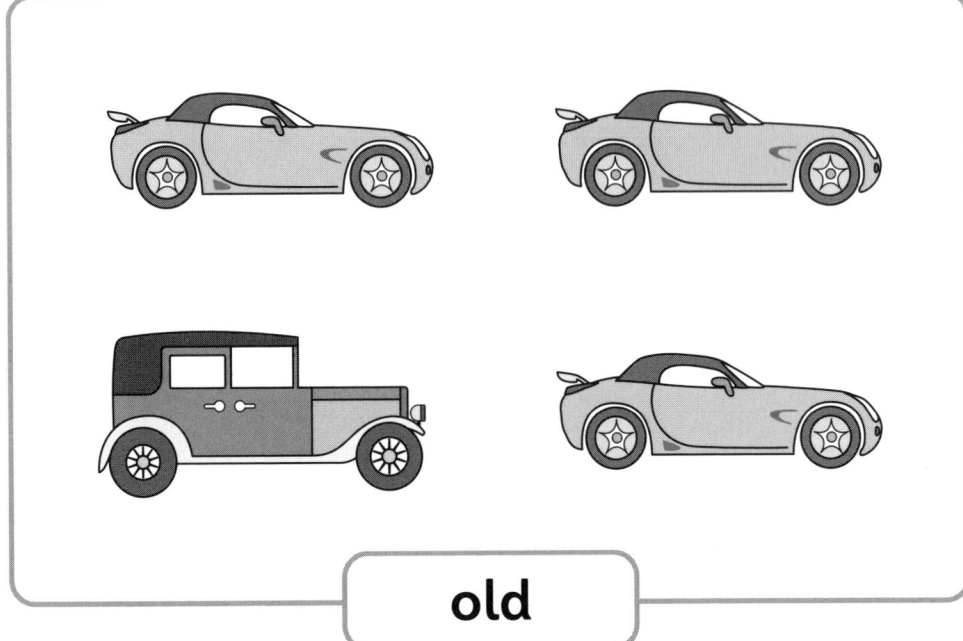

old

slow

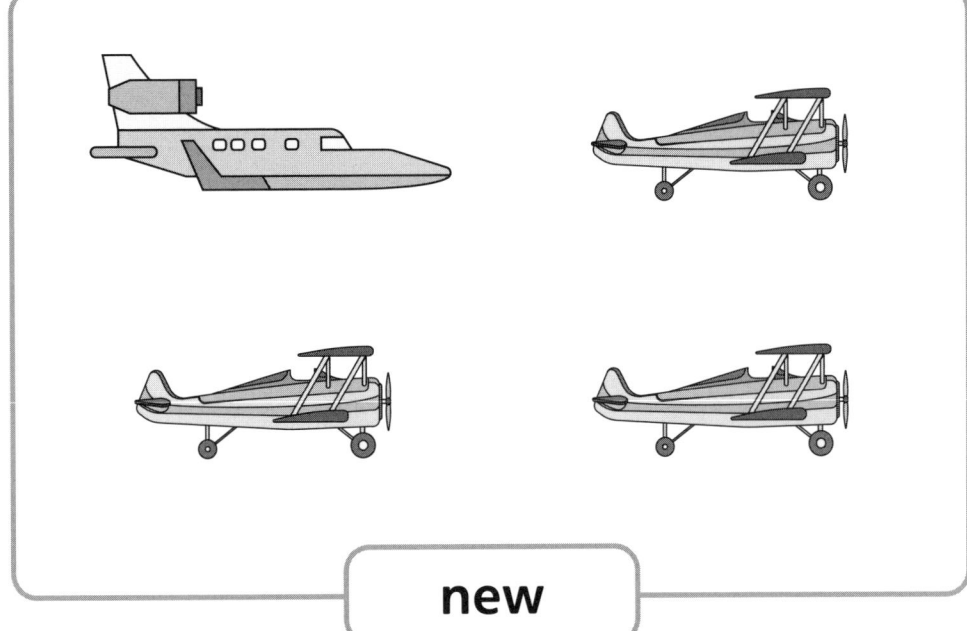

new

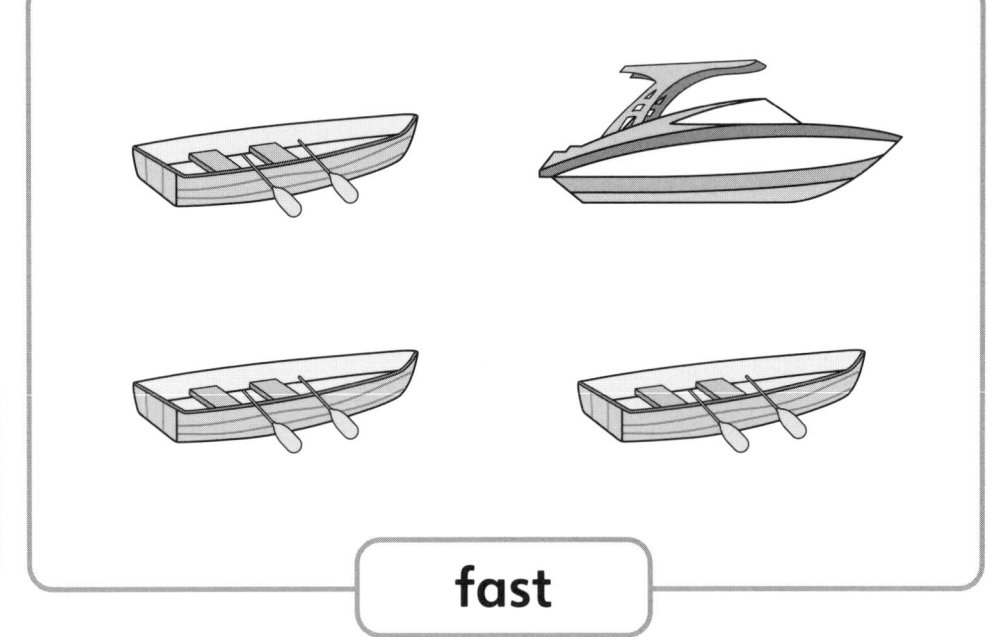

fast

**Concept:** *new / old, fast / slow.* Children look at the pictures in each section. Then, they circle the picture that is different. Finally, children point and say why it's different: *This (car) is (old).*

 **Look.** **Match.** **Say.**

**Vocabulary**

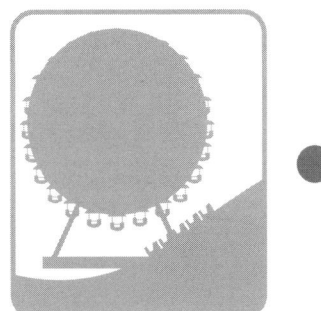

 beach

 amusement park

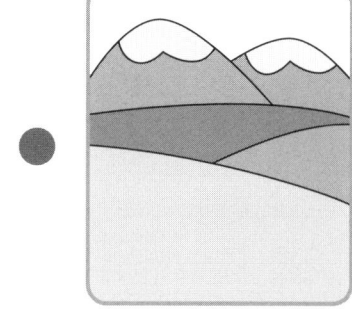 mountains

 city

**Vocabulary:** *beach, amusement park, mountains, city.* Children point to the places in the second column and name each one. Then, they draw lines to match the silhouettes on the left with the places on the right. They then finger trace the lines and name the places as they match the pictures. Finally, children can trace the words.

Unit 8

# Look. Trace. Say.

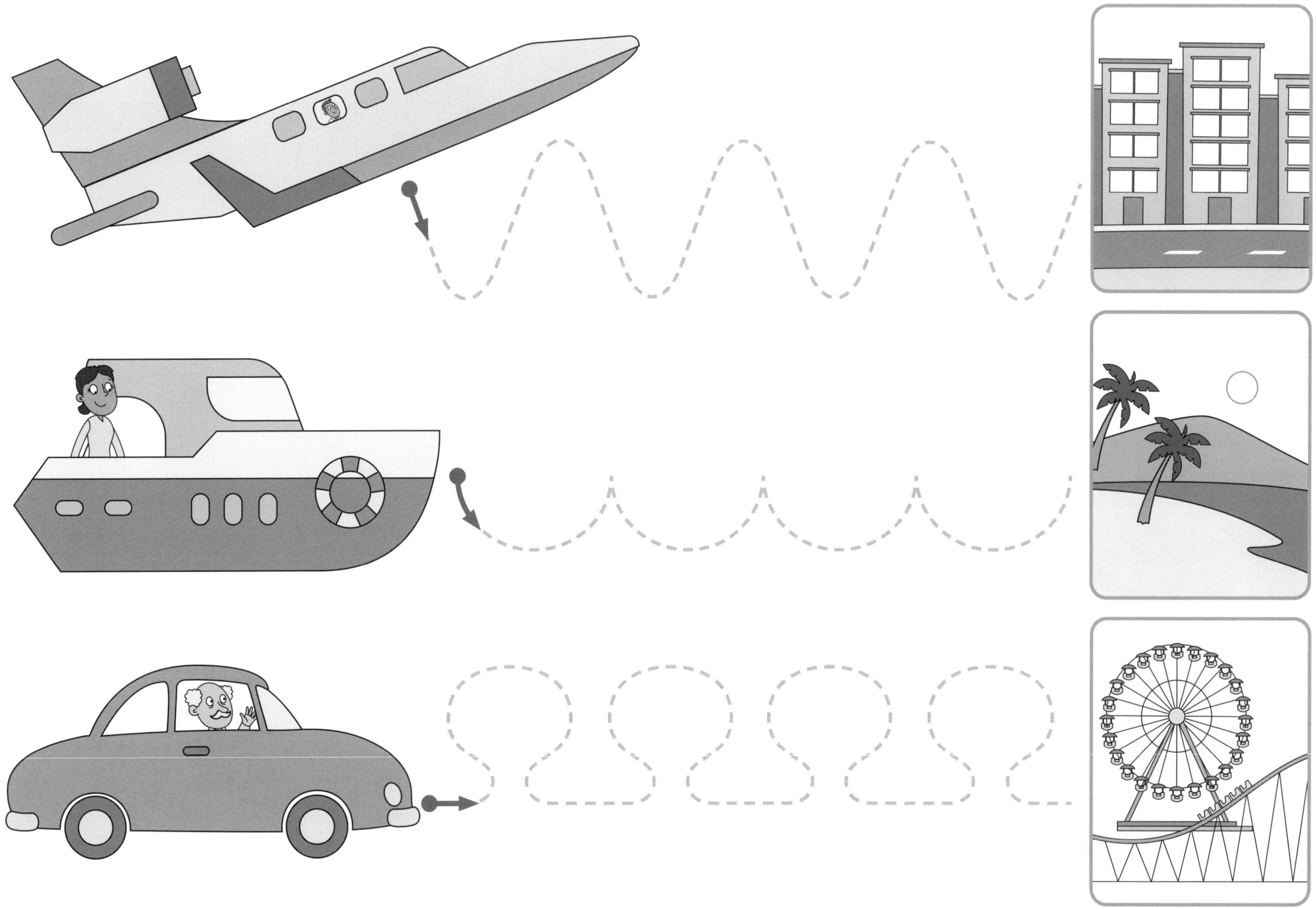

Language

**Language:** *He's / She's going to the (city). He's / She's going to get there (on an airplane).* Children look at the pictures. Point to each of the pictures on the left and ask: *Where's he / she going?* Children trace the line and say: *He's / She's going to the (city).* Then ask: *How's he / she going to get there?* (*He's / She's going to get there on an airplane.*) Children trace all the lines, and point to and describe the pictures.

Unit 8

# ✏️ Draw. 🖍️ Color. 😊 Say.

**Speaking**

**Language:** *This is my (train). It's (yellow).* Ask: *What's your favorite toy?* Encourage children to tell the class what their favorite toy is, and to describe it, e.g., *It's (old). It's (red).* Children draw their favorite toy on the paper on the page, and then complete and color the child to look like themselves. When they finish, children take turns to show their drawing to the class, and describe what they've drawn.

Unit 8

 **Think. Draw. Color. Say.**

**Cross-curricular: Art**

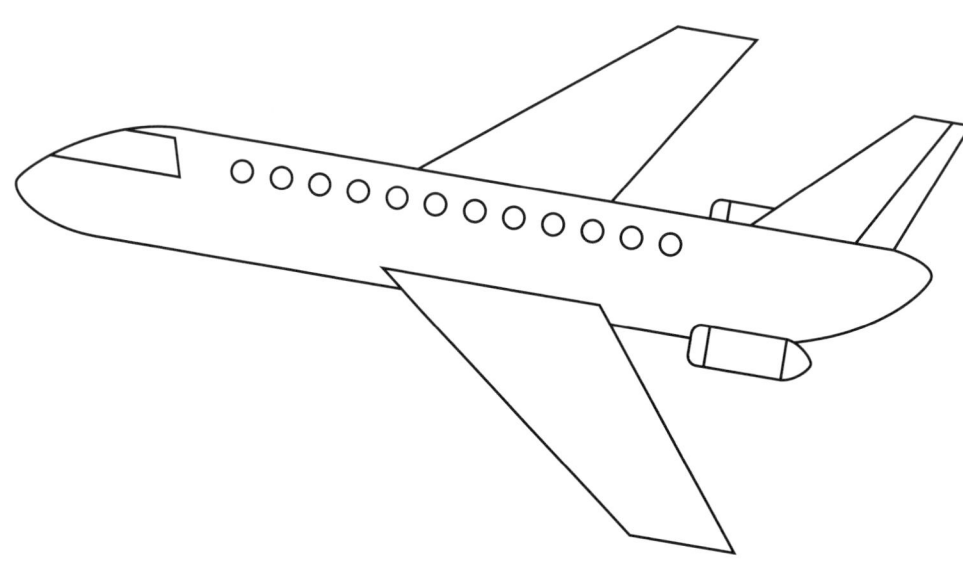

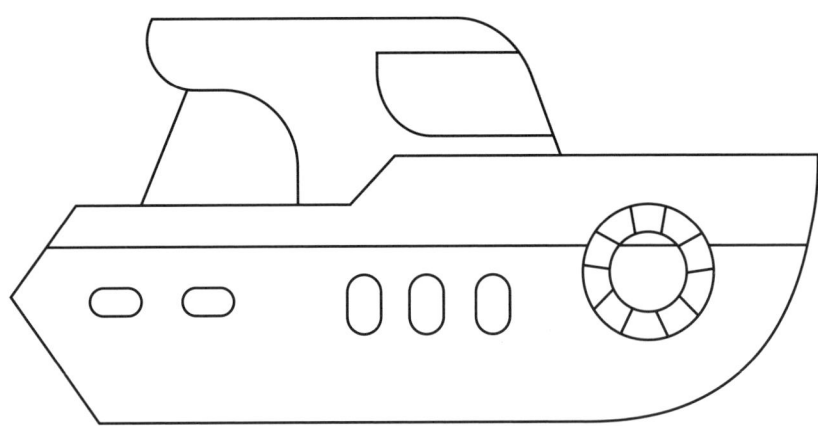

**Art: Using different materials to make art.** Focus on the page and ask children what they can see. Ask them where a boat goes, and where a plane goes. Ask them to imagine what the scenery looks like, and encourage them to share their ideas. Accept all ideas – the more creative, the better! Distribute crayons and children draw their ideas of the scenery around the vehicles. They can also color the vehicles. Alternatively, you could distribute magazines, or colored paper, and children could decorate the vehicles by sticking pieces of paper on them.

123 Count.  Draw.  Trace.   **Numeracy**

10    20    30    40

**Numeracy:** *forty.* Point to the first frame and ask: *How many clouds? Let's count!* Count to 10 together. Children trace 10. Explain that children must draw 10 more clouds in the next frame. When they're finished, ask: *Now how many clouds? Let's count by tens: Ten, twenty!* Children trace 20. Repeat with 30 and 40.

Unit 8 — 113

 Say. Circle. Draw. Color.

Review

## How do we travel?

**My favorite thing in Unit 8:**

**Unit 8**

**Vocabulary and Language Review:** Ask the Big Question: *How do we travel?* Children look back through Unit 8 to recall what they have learned. Ask them to look at the eight pictures from Unit 8. They say the words and then circle the pictures that they are able to name. Then ask: *What was your favorite thing in this unit?* Remind children of the song, story, cross-curricular lesson, etc. They draw a picture of their favorite thing. Children point to and talk about their pictures. Answer the Big Question together, using their pictures as a prompt. Finally, focus on the self-assessment activity. Ask: *How did you do in this unit?* Children color the face that shows how they feel they did.

 # What do plants need to grow?

 Point.  Stick.  Color.  Say.

sun

rain

plant

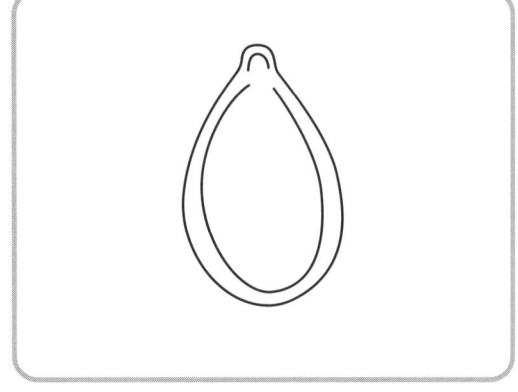

seed

soil

**Vocabulary:** *plant, seed, soil, rain, sun.* Say each new word, and children point to each item as you say it. Say: *(Sun / Rain). Stick the (sun / rain).* Children stick each sticker as you say it. Then name the other items. Children color each item as you say it. They then point to and name each item. Finally, children can trace the words.

 Look. Circle. Color.

Story

  Unit 9

**Language:** *What can you see? bee, daffodil.* Ask children to remember the story. Then ask them to circle five differences between the pictures (in the first picture, there is a bee instead of musical notes, four daffodils, the man is holding up two fingers, the daffodil in the front is sad, the girl has her arms down). Finally, children color the circle of the picture that is from the story.

👁 **Look.** 👄 **Say.** ✨ **Match.** ✏ **Trace.**

**Phonics**

Aa •    • bell •    •

Ee •    • top •    •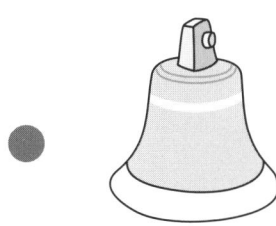

Ii •    • Dad •    •

Oo •    • sun •    •

Uu •    • wig •    •

**Phonics:** *Dad* /æ/, *bell* /e/, *wig* /ɪ/, *top* /ɒ/, *sun* /ʌ/. Point to each letter and say the sound. Children repeat. Repeat with the words and pictures. Point to Aa and ask: *Which word has a?* Show children how to draw lines connecting the letter to the word, and on to the picture. Children draw lines to match each letter, word, and picture. Finally, they follow the letters with their finger, then trace the letters and the words with a pencil.

Unit 9  117

 Look. Match. Say. Color. — Literacy

1.
2.
3.
4.

Do you like the story?

# Look. Say. Color.

Values

**Values: Taking care of plants.** Point to the boy planting a small plant on the table. Ask: *What's he doing? (Taking care of plants.)* Repeat with the other children in the picture. When you come to the girl picking the flower, discuss why it isn't a good idea to pick flowers. Finally, children identify and color the children who are taking care of plants.

Unit 9

# Match. Say. — Vocabulary

shovel

dig a hole

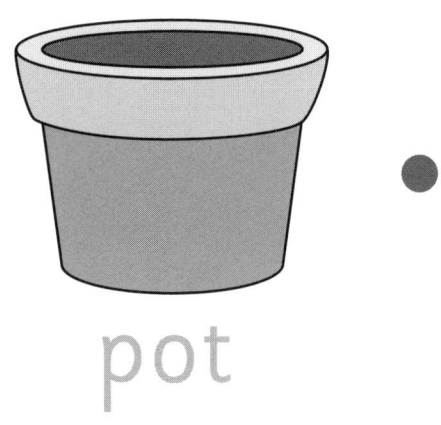
pot

water the seed

watering can

add the soil

**Vocabulary:** *water the seed, dig a hole, add the soil, pot, shovel, watering can.* Point to each object on the left and children say the name. Repeat with the actions on the right. Point to the shovel and ask: *Which action uses a shovel? Water the seed? No...* Children point to *dig a hole*. Repeat with the other pictures. Children draw lines to match the objects to the actions. They point and name each object and action. Finally, children can trace the words and phrases.

👁 **Look.** ✏ **Color.** 😃 **Say.**

**Language**

## 1. First
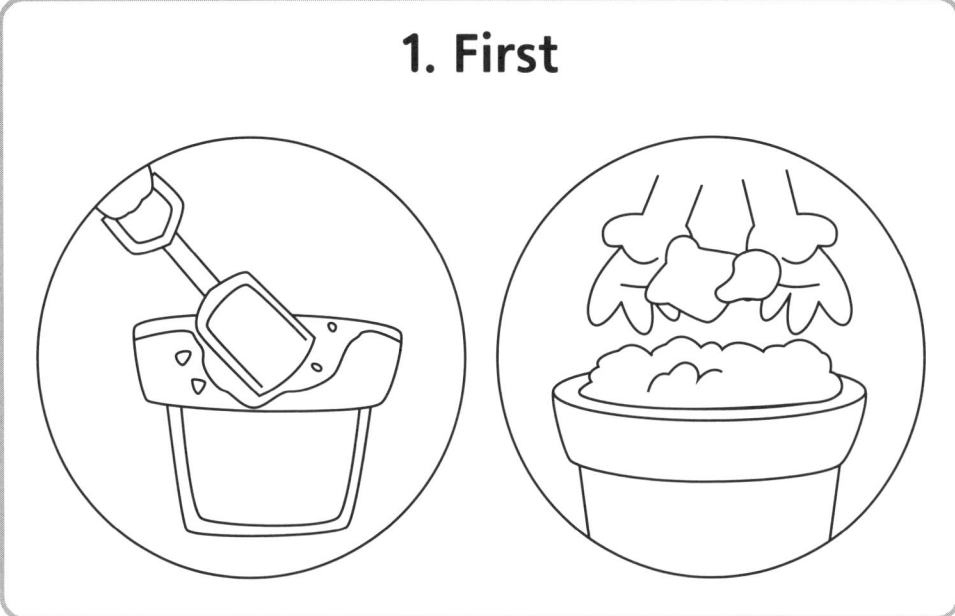

## 2. Next
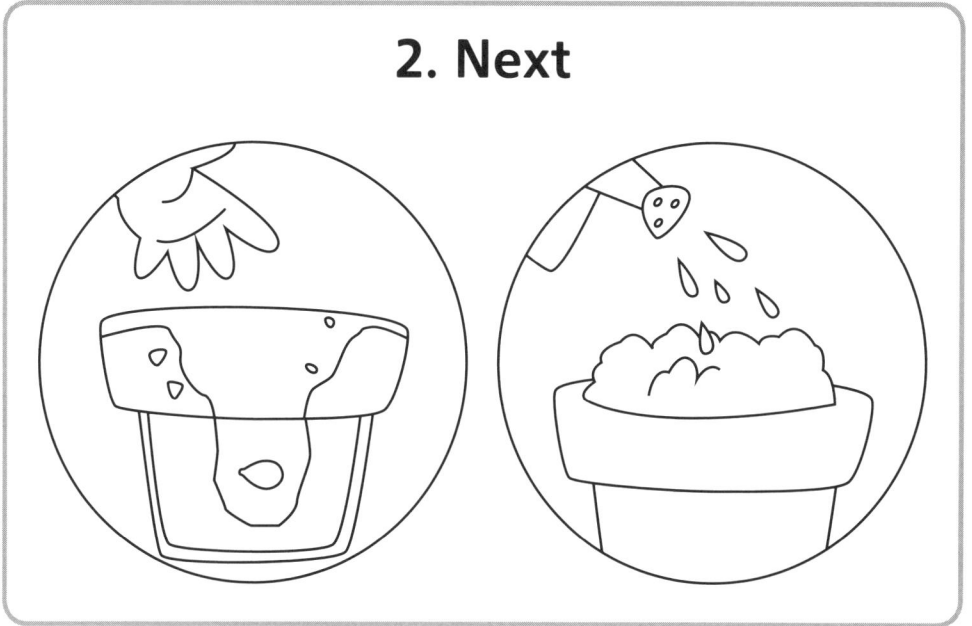

## 3. Then
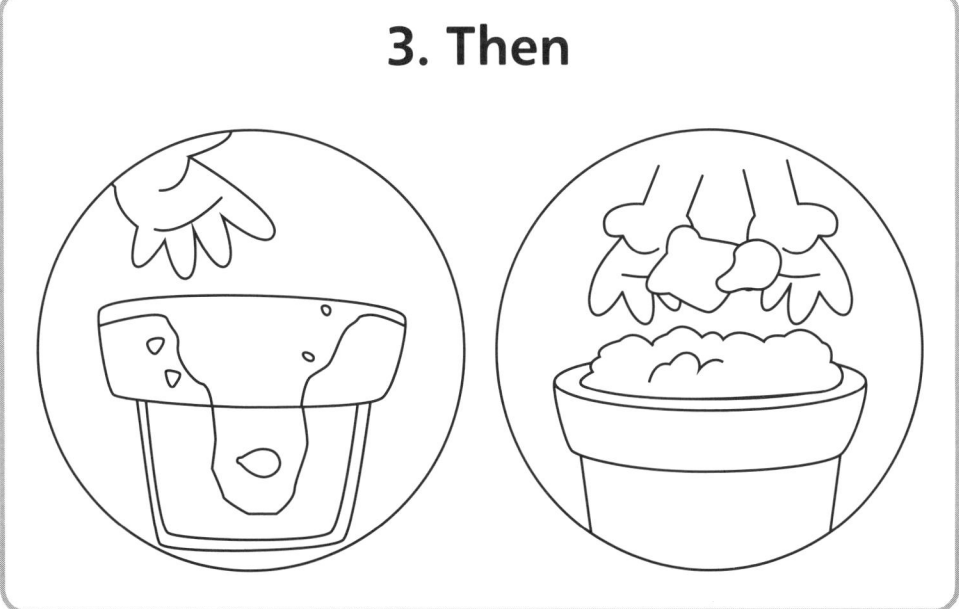

## 4. Finally

**Language:** *(First), (dig a hole).* Look at the first section together. Ask: *What happens first? Dig a hole? Or add the soil?* Discuss and guide children to the correct answer. *(Dig a hole.)* Children color the correct picture. Continue with the other steps: *Add the seed. Add the soil. Water the seed.* Finally, children say the steps in order: *First, dig a hole (with a shovel). Next, add the seed. Then, add the soil. Finally, water the seed (with a watering can.)*

Unit 9

 **Look.**  **Say.**  **Circle.**

Concept

   ?

   ?

   ?

**Concept: *tall / short*.** Children look at each group of pictures on the left of the page. Then, they say the pattern: *Short flower, tall flower, short flower.* Finally, children circle the correct picture on the right to continue the sequence.

Read. Color.

Vocabulary

The petals are red.
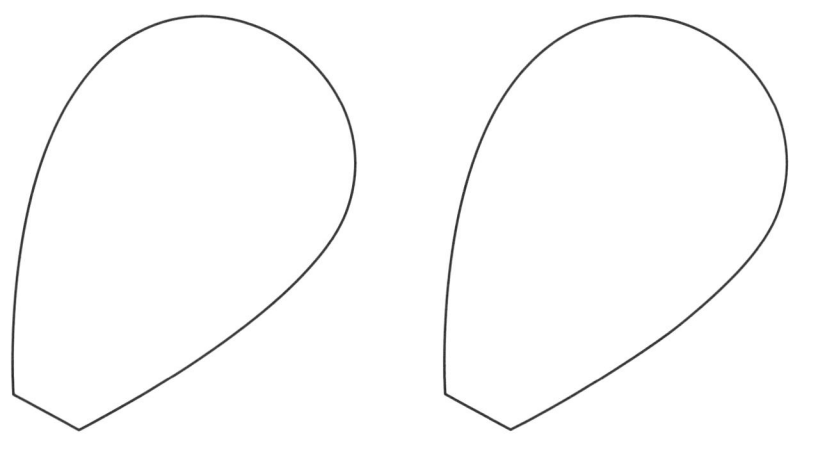

The leaves are green.
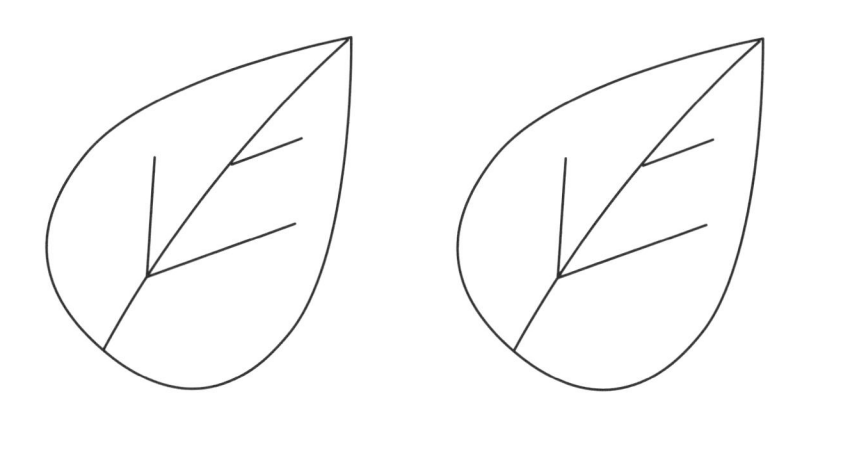

The stem is green.

The roots are brown.
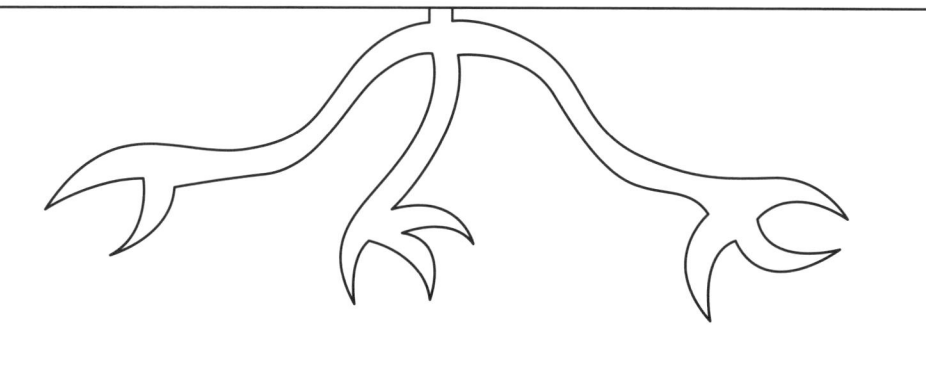

 Look. Say. Draw.

**Language**

**Language: *There's / There isn't a stem. There are some / There aren't any (leaves).*** Point to the first picture, the complete plant. Children name all the flower parts as you point to them: *petals, stem, leaves, roots*. Then, they look at the second picture. Help children to describe the plant and say what's missing: *There are some leaves. There's a stem. There aren't any petals. There are some roots.* Children draw the petals. Continue in this way with the other pictures.

 Say. Draw.

Cross-curricular: Science

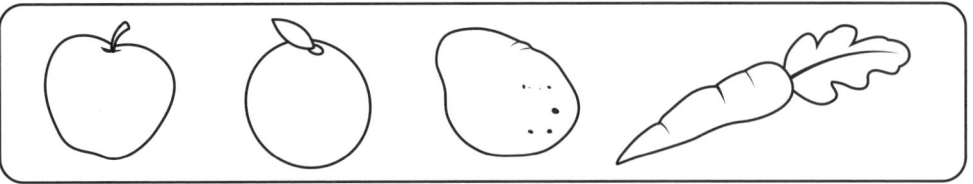

**Science: Learning where fruits and vegetables come from.** Children point to and name the fruits and vegetables at the top of the page (apple, orange, potato, carrot). Point to the apple and ask: *Where do apples grow?* Children point to one of the trees. They draw apples on the tree. Repeat with the other fruits and vegetables. Finally, they point to their pictures and say where the fruits and vegetables grow: *(Oranges) grow (on trees). (Potatoes) grow (underground).*

123 Count.  Trace.  Color.

**Numeracy**

**Numeracy:** *fifty.* Ask: *How many petals on the flowers?* Point to the first flower and say: *Let's count!* Count to 10 together. Continue with the other flowers. Children trace the petals on the last flower. Then say: *How many sets of ten? (Five.) How many petals? Let's count by tens: Ten, twenty, thirty, forty, fifty!* Children trace and say the numbers. Finally, they can color the petals in colors of their preference.

Say. Circle. Draw. Color.

Review

## What do plants need to grow?

**My favorite thing in Unit 9:**

**Unit 9**

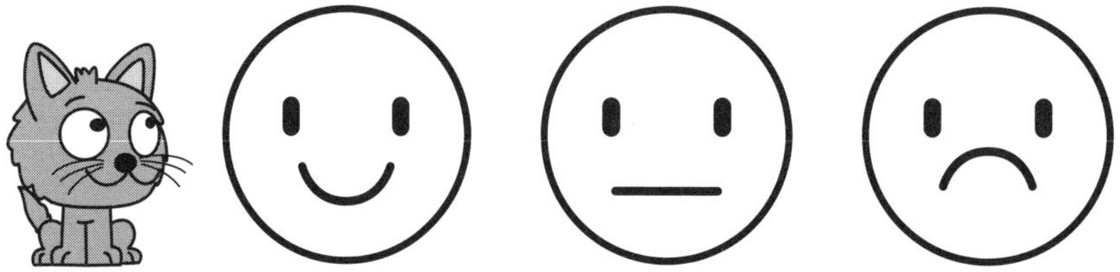

**Vocabulary and Language Review:** Ask the Big Question: *What do plants need to grow?* Children look back through Unit 9 to recall what they have learned. Ask them to look at the eight pictures from Unit 9. They say the words and then circle the pictures that they are able to name. Then ask: *What was your favorite thing in this unit?* Remind children of the song, story, cross-curricular lesson, etc. They draw a picture of their favorite thing. Children point to and talk about their pictures. Answer the Big Question together, using their pictures as a prompt. Finally, focus on the self-assessment activity. Ask: *How did you do in this unit?* Children color the face that shows how they feel they did.

# Picture Dictionary

| Unit 1: Vocabulary 1 | Unit 1: Vocabulary 2 | Unit 1: Vocabulary 3 | Unit 2: Vocabulary 1 |
|---|---|---|---|
| color | glue stick | clean up | brush my hair |
| cut | marker | eat lunch | drink water |
| draw | paintbrush | listen to stories | eat healthy food |
| glue | pencil | play with friends | put on a jacket |
| paint | scissors | sing songs | wash my face |

| Unit 2: Vocabulary 2 | Unit 2: Vocabulary 3 | Unit 3: Vocabulary 1 | Unit 3: Vocabulary 2 |
|---|---|---|---|
| brush | dirty | bathroom | bed |
| jump rope | hungry | bedroom | couch |
| soap | sick | dining room | fridge |
| toothbrush | thirsty | kitchen | lamp |
| towel | tired | living room | shower |

| Unit 3: Vocabulary 3 | Unit 4: Vocabulary 1 | Unit 4: Vocabulary 2 | Unit 4: Vocabulary 3 |
|---|---|---|---|
| cook | cow | collect the eggs | calf |
| make the bed | duck | feed the ducks | chick |
| set the table | hen | groom a horse | duckling |
| sweep the floor | horse | milk a cow | foal |
| watch TV | sheep | shear a sheep | lamb |

## Unit 5: Vocabulary 1

| | |
|---|---|
| breakfast |  |
| chicken |  |
| dinner |  |
| eggs |  |
| lunch | |

## Unit 5: Vocabulary 2

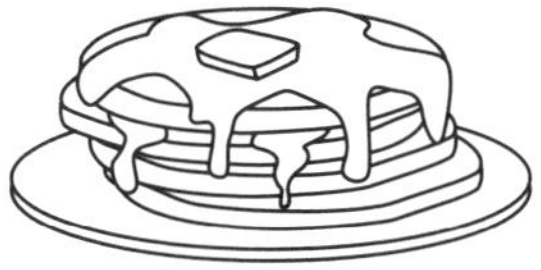

- salad
- pancakes
- rice 
- soup 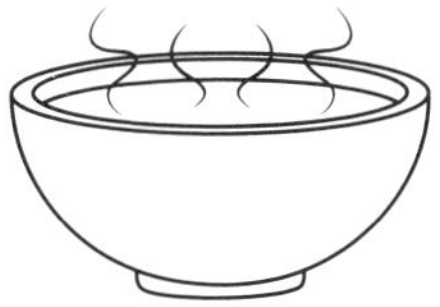
- water 

## Unit 5: Vocabulary 3

- cereal
- fish 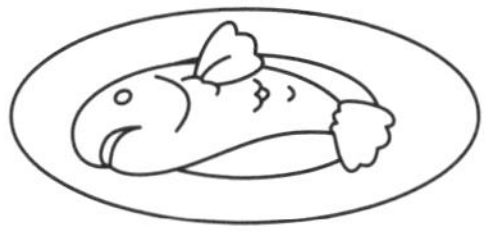
- milk 
- orange juice 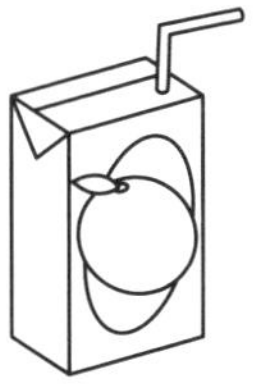
- strawberries 

## Unit 6: Vocabulary 1

- pants
- shoes 
- skirt 
- sweater 
- T-shirt

| Unit 6: Vocabulary 2 | Unit 6: Vocabulary 3 | Unit 7: Vocabulary 1 | Unit 7: Vocabulary 2 |
|---|---|---|---|
| boots | cloudy | hear | bad |
| dress | rainy | see | good |
| jacket | snowy | smell | rough |
| raincoat | sunny | taste | smooth |
| socks | windy | touch | soft |

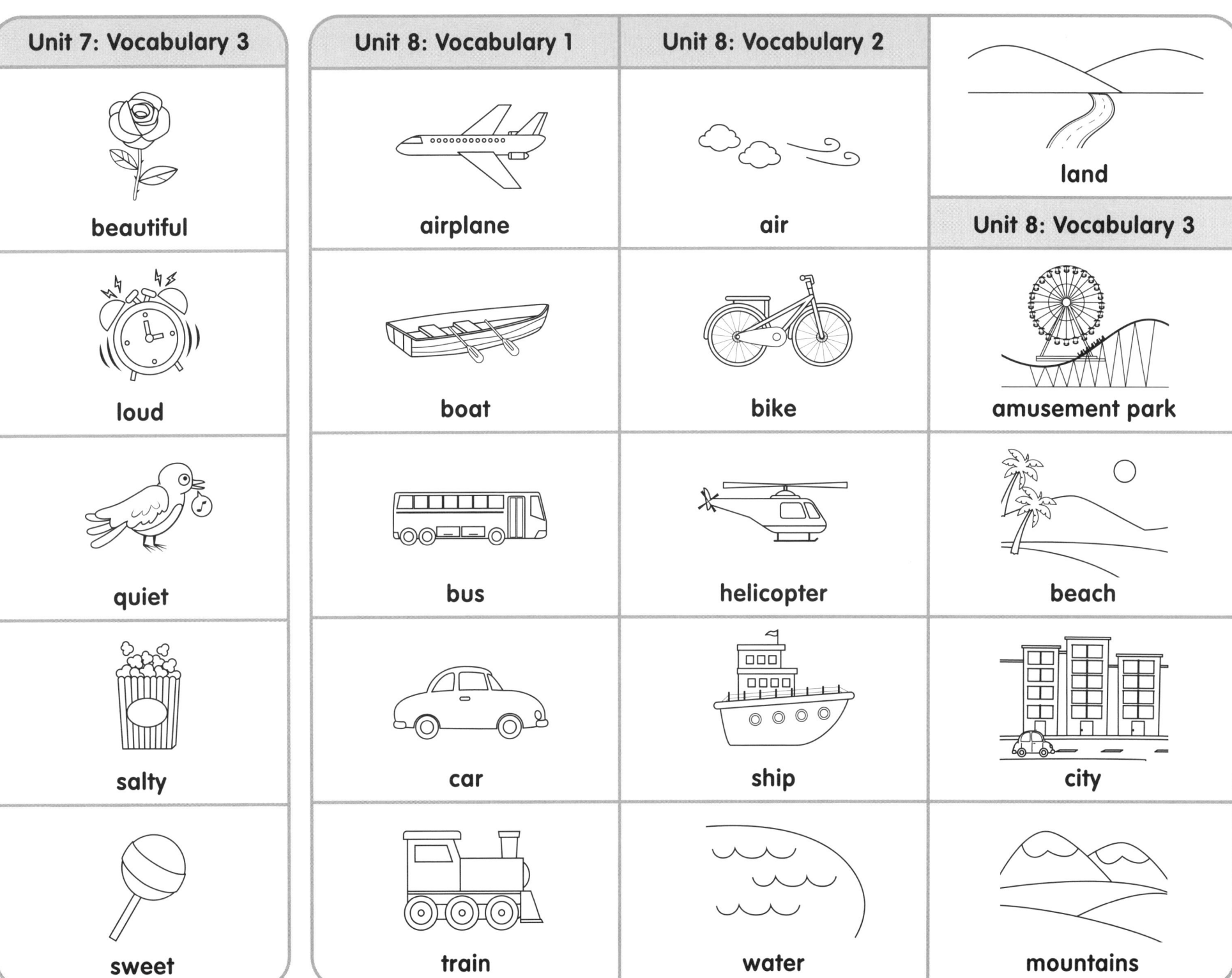

| Unit 9: Vocabulary 1 | Unit 9: Vocabulary 2 | watering can |
|---|---|---|
| plant | add the soil | Unit 9: Vocabulary 3 |
| rain | dig a hole | leaves |
| seed | pot | petals |
| soil | shovel | roots |
| sun | water the seed | stem |

## Unit 1, p. 3

## Unit 2, p. 17

## Unit 3, p. 31

## Unit 4, p. 45

## Unit 5, p. 59

Unit 6, p. 73

Unit 7, p. 87

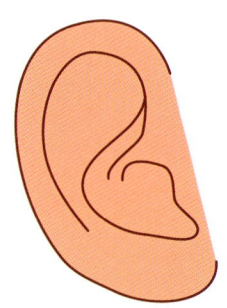

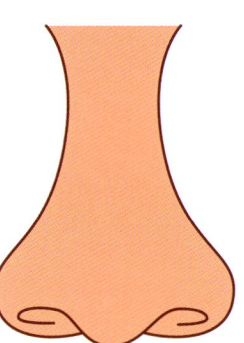

Unit 8, p. 101

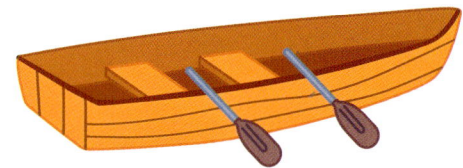

Unit 9, p. 115